A Therapist's Guide to Nonmonogamy

Consensual nonmonogamy (CNM) means that all partners in a relationship consent to expanded monogamy or polyamory. Clinicians are on the front line in providing support for the estimated millions pioneering these modern relationships. This first available guide for therapists provides answers to prevalent questions: What is the difference between expanded monogamy and polyamory? Is CNM healthy and safe? Why would someone choose the complexities of multiple partners? What about the welfare of children? Through illustrative case studies from research and clinical practice, therapists will learn to assist clients with CNM agreements, jealousy, sex, time, family issues, and much more. *A Therapist's Guide to Consensual Nonmonogamy* serves as a step forward toward expanding standard clinical training and helps inform therapists who wish to serve the CNM population.

Rhea Orion is a grandmother, writer, and cancer survivor. She has worked for two decades as teacher, marriage and family therapist, certified sex therapist, and family and consumer scientist.

A Therapist's Guide to Consensual Nonmonogamy

Polyamory, Swinging, and Open Marriage

Rhea Orion

Routledge
Taylor & Francis Group

NEW YORK AND LONDON

First published 2018
by Routledge
711 Third Avenue, New York, NY 10017

and by Routledge
2 Park Square, Milton Park, Abingdon, Oxon OX14 4RN

Routledge is an imprint of the Taylor & Francis Group, an informa business

Library of Congress Cataloging-in-Publication Data
A catalog record for this title has been requested

ISBN: 978-1-138-20745-5 (hbk)
ISBN: 978-1-138-20746-2 (pbk)
ISBN: 978-1-315-46225-7 (ebk)

Typeset in Galliard
by Servis Filmsetting Ltd, Stockport, Cheshire

To Peapod from Lummy
Two halves of the same giddy goddess

Contents

Preface

"Do I have to have sex in my life?" asks Jill plaintively. Shaking her head, she looks and sounds downcast. "I don't want a divorce. Jack and I work well together, and our son is only 5. Other than his being the light of my life, I just want to paint and raise puppies! But I know Jack goes crazy. I believe he doesn't want to cheat, and I *am* his wife."

Jill is a subject in my consensual nonmonogamy (CNM) research. This conversation took place in my office in 2001. Her situation is one of many that can lead to nontraditional relationship formats. I explain to Jill as I do to many clients that there is no empirically determined amount of sex to have or want. There is no scientifically determined frequency of having sex to make a "happy" or "successful" couple. The difficulty for many is the expectation of maintaining a sexually exclusive relationship.

When a couple vows to have sex with no one but each other for the rest of their lives, that's only half the vow. The implicit vow not given much thought is the commitment for each to *be* there to have sex *with*.

Few couples imagine, as they stand at the altar, that their sex life will dwindle and die—assuming they had one to start with. Prior to the late 20th century, proscriptive roles and relationships oppressed women: a condition existing throughout the history of most of the world—and in many locations, it still does. In today's western culture the idea is no longer accepted that a wife must "do her duty" and have sex at her husband's summons. I gladly report that in hundreds of partners I've seen in the past 17 years, I've rarely heard a man say he wants his partner to just roll over and do it, whether s/he wants to or not. Partners of all ilk wish to feel that sex is mutually desired.

Our culture teaches: Find the one right love to marry and everything will work out for a lifetime. That there could be more than one right love is not a mainstream thought. That more than one love can be experienced at the same time, and shared honestly by choice, remains radical thinking, although this idea is becoming more visible and growing more viable. That love is a flowing energy neither owned nor contained sounds like hippie-crystal stuff. But energy flow between minds and hearts is now a topic in advanced scientific circles—as in the ancient Tantric texts.

These radical changes have not existed long in historical terms. It takes time for cultures to catch up with evolution, whether biological or societal, producing what sociologists term *cultural lag*. These developmental advances pose a common problem. Over time and through phases of relationships, sex drive and desire wane and change for both men and women. Few choose to force another to *have* sex, but if one partner is rarely or never there for sex, this is paramount to dooming the other partner *not* to have sex. In essence, this says, *You can't have sex with anyone but me—but I don't want it so you can't have sex at all.* Is forcing someone to have no sex any more acceptable than forcing sex on someone? Most people I've worked with don't think so.

Affairs are understandably experienced as signals of disloyalty and lost love. Extramarital relations ought to be handled honestly. If one is in a monogamous relationship, however, the price of telling the truth is high—possibly even the loss of one's family. The partner who finds love or pleasure outside of marriage might be more disposed to talking about this honestly if alternative ideas were considered: When a relationship expectably changes, this does not mean that love, commitment, or family are over.

A common response to an affair is forcing the offending partner to choose between family and the new person. But you can't un-ring the bell. If genuine love exists between the straying spouse and the outside partner, it's unrealistic to think that cutting off that relationship will either end the love or aid in the repair of the marriage. What if choosing between the two were not the only option?

While not all affairs are examples of unexpected genuine love, we simply must, as a culture, start considering that monogamy is not the only acceptable or moral type of committed relationship. At the least, affairs illuminate issues that may exist in a relationship needing attention. Viewed positively, affairs present opportunities for personal growth and expansion of relationships. Partners, especially if they are also parents, need to consider alternative relationship formats rather than either going straight to separation, or staying together in an atmosphere of mistrust and resentment.

Not all marriages can work, and consensual nonmonogamy is not an answer for everyone, but sex needs to stop being a crucial hinge and the most important component of relationship commitment. Mothers and children must not be at risk because mom and dad, or two moms, or two dads, lose their intimacy. That parents have sex-life changes is a fact of life, which ought not to separate partners and disrupt families.

I am writing this book because I champion love with responsibility in every relationship format. We need to challenge the idea that someone who loves more than one person has a choice only between monogamous sex, or losing the family. CNM clients are pioneers in these new relationships and family-ways and they need help. Therapists need training and information to help all kinds of partnerships, from modern monogamous couples to the rapidly developing alternative of consensual nonmonogamists. University-sponsored CNM research suggests worldwide practice. Therapists need to be riding the crest of this wave.

In addition to providing a surfboard, I hope that this book is as interesting and inspiring as the people in the cases I've shared. I hope that it is easy to use and immediately helpful to my fellow clinicians. I have been truly thankful for each person and partner or set of partners who have shared their journeys with me, and even though their identities are protected here, every one of them has expressed eagerness to be part of changing the clinical and social climate around consensual nonmonogamy.

I know from my research and work that those living in CNM lifeways include families and people from all walks of life, a diversity of race, ethnicity, gender and sexual orientation, and several religions. One of the common complaints unique to this population and brought forth in research is the lack of safe, effective, clinical help. It is my hope that this book will support an increase in the availability of help for consensual nonmonogamists by being a positive response to this needed, inevitable, and unstoppable social change.

Acknowledgments

These acknowledgments hold a disclaimer and a story—

I don't claim to know every term, issue, format, or solution of consensual nonmonogamy (CNM). Although I, and many of my cohorts, were "poly" before there were words for it, I have not consistently kept up with all trends and developments of the CNM world through the decades. My years of study in family, sexual, and psychological sciences and my work with CNM clients inform me about this rapidly evolving lifeway. I am deeply grateful to every person who has shared a complicated, troubled, meaningful, and brave journey with me. Your contribution is here.

Thanks to B, S, Miss Deb, and Anne, for without you I would not know passion, true love, nor friendship. I know why love—platonic or passionate—matters.

I also know what it's like to live nontraditionally. I had many advantages growing up, but too many people died or abandoned us. My family now includes who's left of my blood relatives, my children from different bio-dads, and *fictive kin*—a term used in sociology for those unrelated people who stand by us when they don't have to. And become our family. One member especially, Womark, who joined our family in 1982 because he felt called to. He gave up his plans and dreams to help provide for us, which he has done with word, deed, and dollar ever since, including keeping this book project supplied with printer ink and recycled paper.

There's no label for our family. We're not poly, because none of us have romantic or sexual relationships with each other. A friend used to refer to us as "the hippie family" because few of us are traditionally related by blood or law. We made our own village for raising the children and will take care of each other 'til death do us part. Without this context, I wouldn't be who I am to write this book.

Without my children I'd have known no rapture, nor the unquestionable meaning of life. So I wouldn't be alive.

My mother experienced stigma as a divorced woman in the early 1960s. She always made lemonade out of lemons—and life gave her a lot of lemons. An unsung pioneer of the modern single mother mode, responsible for four daughters, she worked at home editing psychology and medical books for a major publishing house. Active through the civil rights, feminist, hippie, liberal religious, and human potential movements, she became a psychotherapist. Little did we know that these combined life experiences would make this very book possible decades later.

At age 92, my mother is the co-creator of this publication. Without her professional editing skills guided by her insights about humans, love, and therapy, my knowledge would never have organized itself onto readable pages. Her wisdom, suffering, perseverance, mastery, and her love, have brought us all to this event.

Special thanks go to M.P. Smith, who provided a needed second editor's eye, pen, and perspective, and all the folks of the Davis Writer's Salon (especially the lovely, generous hostess, Cindy Keil). The group is always a source of inspiration, motivation, camaraderie, and text correction.

I'm thankful for Mr. Mittens and Bitzka, whose purrs kept me alive in my darkest hours.

I am grateful for the unseen design of my life, and to my publisher, Routledge, for the opportunity to write this book. May it be worthy.

Introduction

Cultural Issues That Matter

As said by my favorite and most influential childhood philosopher, Dr. Seuss, "This may not seem very important I know, but it IS, so I'm bothering telling you so" (Seuss, 1962). The cultural origins and history of marriage may not seem relevant to being an effective therapist with consensual nonmonogamy (CNM) clients, but I explain these same things to almost every person who comes to me for help in a struggling monogamous or CNM relationship. People in CNM relationships may have gathered some of this, because they are moving against it. As therapists, we must understand and question the contexts and norms that significantly impact the life choices people make—and why those choices do and don't work. People are relieved to know, thankful, when their choices and what they consider their failures are placed in a larger context of culture that influences everyone. When they understand that they have been socialized by powerful factors over which they have had no control, they are often relieved of personal guilt. When lack of understanding is replaced by enlightened perspective, self-esteem benefits.

Consensual nonmonogamy is a newly acknowledged growing phenomenon in the western world. The blog, "Polyamory in the News" by "Alan M" recently posted a National Public Radio article, "A cultural moment for polyamory" (King, 2017), which discusses the continued growth and public awareness of consensual nonmonogamy. CNM challenges the acceptance and safety of "normal." Just as it has been important to develop science to accept that a variety of gender and sexual orientations are in fact "normal," so is it important to understand the differences between traditional monogamy, expanded monogamy, polyamory, and all forms of consensual nonmonogamy. This calls for refamiliarizing ourselves with the cultural and historical aspects of marriage and family. It is important with many clients to familiarize them with these realities.

Professed monogamy has been the accepted mainstream norm for centuries in western culture, but mainstream life in the world has actually been different. The reasons why couples in the past stayed together for a lifetime likely had less to do with happiness and frequent sex, than law. There has always been adultery; it's just that for men it was accepted even where considered untoward. Women, on the other hand, have been branded, left with starving bastard children, stoned to death, or beheaded—even for submitting with no choice. Once married, happiness was not a requirement. Law-enforced duty—obedience of the wife—prevailed. Sex was not even discussed. So historically, monogamy has been supported by necessity.

In 1917, only 100 years before this book is being written, the realities of marriage still reflected the history of the western world. The average lifespan was 48 years (Berkeley.edu, 2017; Elderweb.com, 2017). *'Til death do us part* was then a much shorter time. Marriage was necessary for survival for both women and children. Women had as many babies as possible, as it was likely some would die. Wife and children were legally the property of the husband. Laws prevented divorce. Marriage lasted because alternatives were rare and not widely available. There were few ways out and few ways to survive without marriage. But marriage was almost always for a shorter lifetime than is now ordinary; recent science and technology have nearly doubled human lifespan expectancy.

That love is involved in marriage has been an ideal for centuries, but perhaps rarely experienced. Certainly our society provides no tools for carrying out this ideal. Today media is our most powerful and widespread teacher and still promotes the fairy tale: We simply have to meet that one right person, love each other enough, and we'll live happily ever after.

Monogamy does work for some people, but it needs to become common knowledge that success is not automatic just because two people love each other. Nearly all partners in any relationship format are currently flying by the seat of their pants, trying to figure out how to make things work in a very changed world—without enough changed information.

Monogamy needs updating. Little is offered culturally that helps modern couples make a success of traditional marriage. Other models are a response to cultural evolution; consensual nonmonogamy is part of this process. Research shows that CNM relationships, including polyamory, are as successful, or not, as is monogamy (Emens, 2003; Orion, 2010; Sheff, 2014; Sheff, personal interview, September 23, 2017). Tools, information, and support that can be provided in therapy are sometimes needed for either model to work well.

The acceptance of change in the legal requirement of the sex of married partners (from one MAN and one WOMAN to including same-sex marriage) has triggered expanded clinical awareness and training. So far, the numerosity requirement (ONE man/woman and ONE man/woman) has not become an issue fought widely on the legal level for acceptance, but responsible multipartnering, including LGBTQIQ (Lesbian, Gay, Bisexual, Transgender, Queer, Intersex, Questioning) persons and families, is on the rise and growing into a significant population (Cloud, 1999; Emens, 2003; Haupert, Gesselman, Moors, Fisher, & Garcia, 2016; King, 2017; Lovemore.com, 2007; Orion, 2008a, 2008b, 2010).

Some people can and do have lifelong, happy, sexually monogamous relationships. My experience and conclusions from research and history cause me to believe it is a minority of modern couples who can or will do so. In addition to cultural reasons, there is growing common knowledge in the field of sexology that *monogamous* or *polyamorous* may be forms of natural sexual orientation existing on a range from sexually monogamous to sexually open.

Consensual nonmonogamy also exists across a range of types: from private arrangements where partners have permission but don't know details about each other's outside partners, to multiple partnerships so open that all live together as "spouses." Most have to keep their arrangements secret from the public and often from family, friends, and employers, but the openness of formats within relationships and families varies greatly along the continuum.

Many problems needing therapeutic intervention exist regardless of whether a person or partners are in a CNM relationship. Dealing with more than one relationship openly and responsibly does have unique challenges, however. My research (Orion, 2008a, 2008b) reveals that time management, communication, jealousy, stigma, and difficulty in locating safe, effective help are among the top complaints of those in CNM relationships.

With the exception of stigma and scarcity of help, these problems are also seen frequently in traditional monogamous relationships. When we multiply feelings, communication, and time management issues by however many partners there are, these issues are magnified in CNM arrangements and may require additional preparation by clinicians.

When a Specialist Is Necessary

When CNM clients seek help with a general therapist for sexual issues, addressing other relational aspects such as those commonly presented to clinicians may resolve the sex problems. If not, a referral to a *certified* sex therapist must be made. At the time of this writing, training in sexual diagnoses and treatment, i.e., sex therapy, is completely lacking for general therapists, marriage and family therapists, psychologists, medical doctors, and social workers (Asher, 2007; Clark, 2009; Orion, 2010). If clients even mention their sexual problems in general therapy, these problems often remain unaddressed, or worse, are handled incorrectly. Since sexology training for clinicians and physicians is nonexistent, it is understandable that these practitioners are not fully aware of the vast field of sex therapy and how much there is to learn. Some clinicians may know a great deal about helping former sexual abuse victims, for example. This is not the same as certification knowledge. Most specifically sexual issues brought to therapy require a referral to a qualified sex therapist, at least for a consultation to provide a brief assessment and an additional opinion. Therapists do not diagnose medical conditions, but refer the client out. Physicians do not counsel patients on relationship problems. It may seem like "just sex" and that sex issues will resolve when other dynamics are addressed, but often this is not true. Sexuality needs to be addressed directly and with specialized approaches, tools, and information. In addition, medical issues may be involved that clinicians have no knowledge of, but about which sex therapists are trained to ascertain and make appropriate referrals.

A certified sex therapist has completed hundreds of hours of coursework and supervised counseling specifically in sexual issues, *after* attaining a general therapy license. Trained sex therapists are specialists and have a distinct set of tools for diagnoses and treatment of common and difficult problems. Sexuality clinicians must keep up with science and application in the field of sexology as well as continuing education in their licensure field.

At this time few programs exist that provide certification in the United States, and no license or laws exist regulating the use of the title "sex therapist," except in Florida. I have heard many well-meaning clinicians refer to themselves as sex therapists because they developed a practice that includes treating one or more sexual problems, but who are not trained or certified in that field. Their intentions are to help clients, but they are unaware that they are missing a vast field of knowledge. This lack puts clients at risk. Training requirements for licensure in several fields need to be expanded, but until they are, when making a referral, please check for specific sexology credentials. Training in sex therapy is comprehensive and it matters. A zip code listing of certified sex therapists can be found on the website of the American Association of Sex Educators, Counselors, and Therapists: AASECT.org.

What This Book Offers

My academic qualitative research (2007, 2008a, 2010) on consensual non-monogamy has informed my work with the CNM population and the overall content of this book. Revealed by the research (and 17 years of working with CNM partners) are inherent issues, problems, and resolutions; pros and cons of CNM; types of arrangements partners make, and advice they would give to others.

Part I contains academically oriented information about how monogamy has changed and about consensual nonmonogamy. This includes language used in CNM circles; what CNM is not, including common social and clinical misconceptions; and what CNM is.

Part II delves into common issues and interventions, including excerpts from selected cases with discussion. Examples chosen illustrate why CNM works for some, not for others, and highlight the many and varied complexities that impact therapy with this population. Issues and interventions presented range from jealousy to time management to physical and mental health issues. Slotted in between the chapters of Part II are summarized case excerpts of people in various types of CNM partnerships, and of monogamous couples who tried and succeeded, or failed, at CNM. Each case is followed by a brief discussion of points relevant to therapeutic intervention.

Important disclaimer: Even if a story sounds like you or someone you know—your aunt, neighbor, co-worker, or friend—it is not! To protect the privacy of research participants and clients, I have changed not only names, but also occupations, locations, and other details. Some cases described are composites of more than one similar example. The issues, feelings, situations, and clinical interventions are accurately presented, however.

Training received by most therapists is adequate for addressing common personal and relationship issues. Presented with CNM issues, however, research has identified at least three primary problems in therapeutic settings: lack of knowledge, client marginalization, and therapist bias (Heinrich & Trawinski, 2016; Weitzman, 1999, 2006). This book offers a comprehensive look inside the lives of polyamorists and other consensual nonmonogamists. Understanding clients' emotions and experiences is crucial to addressing these therapeutic gaps and developing effective assistance.

As with any group considered "abnormal," polyamorists and persons in other CNM lifeways have experienced judgment from families, communities, and institutions. Therapists must expand cultural competency to help reduce stigmatization and provide a safe therapeutic environment. Those new to serving CNM clients can become aware of and hone metaskills: "deeply held feeling attitudes expressed by the therapist through how they say and do things" (Heinrich & Trawinski, 2016). Examining feelings and attitudes about CNM lifeways, which may be unfamiliar and possibly jarring, helps clinicians to be more open without passing judgment on the issues and experiences of consensually nonmonogamous persons. Heinrich and Trawinski (2016) state that the metaskills of "acceptance, curiosity, open mindedness, celebration of diversity and willingness to explore relationship configurations," are necessary to counsel CNM clients, and are "arguably the ethical obligation of the clinician."

This book provides information missing from most clinical training about CNM lifeways, the issues that CNM clients face and may bring to therapy, insight on applying therapeutic approaches to problems unique to CNM, and when to make a referral. It is my hope that this manual is interesting, informative, and immediately useful to clinicians.

References

Asher, R. L. (2007). Has training in human sexuality changed over the past twenty years? A survey of clinical psychology, counseling psychology, and doctor of social work programs. (Doctoral dissertation, Spaulding University, Louisville, KY). Retrieved February 21, 2009, from Dissertations & Theses: Full Text database (Publication No. AAT 3297140).

Berkeley.edu (2017). Lifespan demographics. Available at: http://u.demog.berkeley.edu/~andrew/1918/figure2.html

Clark, J. (2009). Psychology students: Learn to talk about sex. *GradPsych*, 7(2), 8.

Cloud, J. (1999, November 15). Henry & Mary & Janet & . . . Is your marriage a little dull? The "polyamorists" say there's another way. *Time, 154*(20), 90–91.

Elderweb.com, 2017. Lifespan demographics. Available at: www.elderweb.com/book/appendix/1900-2000-changes-life-expectancy-united-states/

Emens, E. F. (2003). Monogamy's law: Compulsory monogamy and polyamorous existence. Working Paper No. 58. Chicago: Chicago Law School.

Haupert, M., Gesselman, A., Moors, A., Fisher, H., & Garcia, J. (2016). Prevalence of experiences with consensual non-monogamous relationships: Findings from two nationally representative samples of single Americans. *Journal of Sex & Marital Therapy*, doi: 10.1080/0092623X.2016.1178675.

Heinrich, R. & Trawinski, C. (2016). Social and therapeutic challenges facing polyamorous clients. *Sexual and Relationship Therapy*, doi: 10.1080/14681994.2016.1174331.

King, B. J. (2017, March 23). A cultural moment for polyamory. NPR article posted by "Alan M," blog Polyamory in the News at polyinthemedia.blogspot.com

Lovemore.com. (2007). Retrieved October 17 from www.lovemore.com/faq.shtm

Orion, R. (2007). *Polyamory and the bisexual marriage.* Research report. San Francisco: Saybrook Graduate School and Research Center.

Orion, R. (2008a). *From traditional to open marriage.* Case study report. San Francisco: Saybrook Graduate School & Research Center.

Orion, R. (2008b). Polyamory as treatment for low desire. Paper presented at the Western Regional Conference of the Society for the Scientific Study of Sexuality, April, 2008, San Diego, CA.

Orion, R. (2010). Unhappily ever after: Examining definitions and treatments of low desire and low-sex relationships. Dissertation, Saybrook University, San Francisco.

Seuss, Dr. (1962). *The sleep book.* New York: Random House.

Sheff, E. A. (2014). *The polyamorists next door: Inside multiple relationships and families.* Lanham, MD: Rowman & Littlefield.

Weitzman, G. D. (1999, March). What psychology professionals should know about polyamory: The lifestyles and mental health concerns of polyamorous individuals. Paper presented at 8th Annual Diversity Conference, Albany, NY.

Weitzman, G. D. (2006). Therapy with clients who are bisexual and polyamorous. *Journal of Bisexuality, 6* (1–2), 137–164, doi: 10.1300/J159v06n01_08.

Part I
Definitions and Social Issues

1   The Magical Story of Monogamy

Consensual nonmonogamy, a term developed over several decades of growing practice, is an emerging model responding to human and cultural change. To understand *non*monogamy, we must understand monogamy and what has happened culturally to bring about its opposite.

Traditional monogamous marriage is hinged on that formal vow of complete faithfulness. "Without the sex," I hear frequently from couples whose sex life has disappeared, "what's the difference between being married and being roommates?"

The nuclear family is a model that emerged during the Baby Boomer years: a heterosexual couple and their biological children, one spouse employed outside the home and the other a full-time caretaker. Some estimates are that as few as 13% of families actually live this way. As of the year 2000, stepfamilies are the most common form; there is no typical family (Mackay, 2000; Strong & DeVault, 1992).

Despite well-known statistics on the prevalence of divorce, millions of couples a year flock to the altar, in white gowns and tuxedos, to say vows. A "halo effect" surrounding monogamy in American culture supports the perpetuation of desire and positive regard for monogamous relationship structures (Conley, Moors, Matsick, & Ziegler, 2013; Moors, Matsick, Ziegler, Rubin, & Conley, 2013). Weddings are very big business. Details vary, but whether implicit or explicit, *sexual monogamy 'til death do us part* remains the crux of being wed. Sick or well, rich or poor, we also vow to stand by one another. But if either partner breaks the vow of exclusivity—that often overrides the contract and leads to divorce.

At least in modern times, that is. Historically, men got away with a lot of cheating, but women, as the legal property of the husband, did not. Whether a couple had sex or how often was not a topic of discussion. It was the female's duty, the man's presumed need and right.

Thanks to massive cultural changes brought about by feminism and hippies, this forced sexual monogamy and double standard are not even remembered by a couple of generations. Unless they study history of marriage and family, today's young couples would be shocked if they had to go back and live in an earlier era.

The modern idea of marriage, or "supermonogamy" (Emens, 2004), is a powerful fairy tale permeating our society. With the freedom and equality brought about by social evolution, one might think that being married would bring less pressure, that requirements would be relaxed. Instead, the list of expectations inherent in the modern marriage has grown considerably: Not only is sexual exclusivity still a mainstream expectation, but sex is supposed to be desired equally, to be frequent and exciting with numerous orgasms for both partners.

As the modern nuclear couple who can do it all, spouses are both expected to work and manage careers, buy homes, be parents, and take care of elders, for as long as the seventy-plus years either spouse may now live. This supermonogamy is current socialization, yet there is nothing in science or nature to suggest that these expanded expectations can be fulfilled.

We don't see what happens after the wedding when Cinderella and the prince arrive in the bedroom. If Cinderella has sexual pain or the prince has erectile dysfunction, if either one is gay or polyamorous by nature, what then? Our media princess models have improved, providing us with female warriors and leaders who save others and have complex powerful jobs. Their princes may or may not have advanced much from traditionally depicted roles, but the idea still stands that once together with *the right one*, everything will be great forever.

What if there is a likely deterioration of this ideal couple's sex life? Or they just don't get along as well as they thought they would, now that they're married? The prince wants a family but Cinderella feels overwhelmed with children and wifely duties. Maybe they could both use a second spouse as part of the equation! (When does such a movie plot come out?) Research and evidence suggest that millions of people worldwide are actually living that plot, whether or not it is discussed, accepted, or depicted (Cloud, 1999; Emens, 2004; Haupert, Gesselman, Moors, Fisher, & Garcia, 2016; King, 2017; Lovemore.com, 2007; Orion, 2008a, 2011). This is emerging cultural change.

Monogamous marriage is a powerful story full of magic. Research shows that in modern America *the couple* is prioritized as one of the most important relationships in one's life, and it is presumed that nearly everyone desires monogamy (Day, Kay, Holmes, & Napier, 2011; DePaulo & Morris, 2005; Haupert, et al., 2016). Monogamy once meant survival and was prescribed by religion and law. People are no longer forced into this mode. But many believe in the Cinderella magic and follow that dream. Since it is clear that this model of marriage so often doesn't work, what magic is the ongoing power of the story?

Though laws have changed somewhat and various religions and spiritual movements now abound, there remains a natural desire to pair bond: a powerful instinct to mate and create a secure nest. Love is necessary to survival—and makes living worthwhile. Who wants to face loneliness, pain, and loss? Or feel unsafe or insecure? The magic of the story of monogamy is that it promises what we need and prevention of loss—all while having sex with a mate one can count on!

This is a wonderful, humane story! Who wouldn't want it to come true? Unfortunately, it so often proves untrue. It is not the right story for everyone.

It is a tale based neither on science nor on nature. The Cinderella magic is the residue of thousands of years of patriarchy, of no separation between church and state, and of our human tendency to carry on in adulthood as childhood taught.

Modern couples are potentially pioneering the development of new models for successful relationships and familyways. Today's monogamous couples seek love-based, egalitarian monogamy by *choice*, not by force or law; we might call this *consensual monogamy*, as opposed to the forced and unquestioned monogamy of western history. Carrying out this choice requires information, hard work, communication skills, establishment of rules and boundaries, personal growth, time, energy, maintenance of intimacy, and commitment. This is the same list required for carrying out successful *non*traditional partnerships. Both are legitimate and viable models for modern life. Traditional relationships are changing; new relationship formats are emerging, including new models of monogamy.

My experience is that many committed sexually monogamous couples are unwittingly relying on what they think is normal human behavior, based on their cultural upbringing. But neither instinct nor socialization supports fulfillment of high modern marital expectations.

Problems exist when couples marry without having the tools to successfully carry out modern choices and requirements. Our culture offers no mandatory education on relationship skills, sexuality, child development, parenting, or family life, because the story continues: With that one right person, life is a happy ending. Unfortunately, the story *is* a magical fairy tale. Love is not all we need for successful relationships.

Through research and clinical experience, I learned that the most common complaint brought to therapists and several types of physicians is the low and no-sex relationship. The waning of desire and sexual activity is common for individuals and for committed couples and has a myriad of causes (Orion, 2011). This is not dysfunction—this is the norm. Modern consensual monogamy is still hinged on a factor of desire and sexual activity. This aspect of relationships is unreliable, and automatic genuine sexual chemistry cannot be manufactured.

Monogamy, according to Merriam-Webster dictionary is:

(1) The practice or state of being married to one person at a time.
(2) The practice or state of having a sexual relationship with only one partner.
(3) *Zoology*: The habit of having only one mate at a time.

The term *monogamy* is used by virtually everyone and is socially and legally considered the mainstream acceptable form of relationship upon which our complex culture is founded. Monogamy is one of the Fundamental American Family Values, yet several issues complicate clear understanding of what monogamy actually is.

Advances in various sciences present the current knowledge about monogamy:

- Monogamy is not global but is a *socialized* cultural norm.
- Monogamy is proclaimed to be, but is not the actual *practiced* cultural norm.

- Monogamy is not instinctive for humans.
- Monogamy is not defined the same by everyone.
- Monogamy is not the only workable, loving choice.

Monogamy Is Not Global but Is a *Socialized* Cultural Norm

From womb to adulthood, our experience of being conceived, born, and brought up in our family of origin profoundly impacts our sexuality and relationships. Add in the powerful social influences of where and when any person is born and raised, and we may get the full recipe for what creates any individual's sex and relationship predilections.

Our culture continues to be socially programmed by family, schools, and by media—religious and secular sources alike—that *one person for a lifetime* is the ideal. The assumption is that this works for others and is the historic successful norm, therefore all couples should know automatically how to make it work. A happy lifetime together, including sexual exclusivity, is the dream. The magical fairy tale.

Many times I've heard disgruntled couples say, when their own fairy tale gets holes in it, "My parents stayed together and I want to," or "I know couples who are still together after twenty or thirty years, isn't that what's supposed to happen?" Many are in serious, deep emotional pain, bashing themselves as failures because they can't make their traditional sexually monogamous relationship work. They blame themselves, not realizing their understandable lack of knowledge and tools, and not realizing they are expecting magic.

Monogamy Is Proclaimed to Be, but Is Not the Actual *Practiced* Cultural Norm

Mackay (2000) reports statistics that remain throughout western cultures where monogamy is the mainstream style of marriage: in 40–80% of relationships at least one partner cheats at least once. Mackay's report includes information from the World Health Association: In the year 2000, among sexually active 16–45-year-olds in six nations including America, between 22 and 50% of adults reported being sexually unfaithful (these are just the subjects who admit it). Observation of current culture does not reveal improvement.

The most common relationship in western civilization is now *serial monogamy*— one monogamous relationship after another. Webster's dictionary's definitions of monogamy include the habit of having only one mate, or being married to only one person at a time. According to this standard, many may be monogamous for a lifetime, even though they change partners along the way.

Monogamy Is Not Instinctive for Humans

In virtually every scientific field, humans are revealed to resemble most species in existence, as *non*monogamous by nature. Current sexology posits whether a tendency toward or away from sexual monogamy lies on a continuum. Some people may, by nature, not be suited for, or desirous of, more than one mate. Others may be naturally drawn to multiple sexual partners at any given time, and often to more than one exclusive sexual partner—each for a period of years— during a lifetime.

Sexuality is instinctive. Survival is our strongest instinct and sexual monogamy is rare among all creatures on the planet. According to Buss (2017), only 3% of mammalians have long-term, committed mating, in part because monogamy does not ensure survival (Ferrer, 2007). For example, some birds "mate for life." They come back to the same partner year after year at mating season. Because of DNA testing, however, we now know that every third to fifth egg is fertilized by a different male. Why? In case her chosen mate's eggs do not survive for some genetic reason, the female bird will still have offspring.

Survival of the species is a powerful part of what sex and relationships are all about! Humans, however, have evolved into wanting and being capable of more than socialized monogamy and mating instinct as bases for partnerships and families (Buss, 2017; Ferrer, 2007; Fisher, 2016; Gray & Garcia, 2013; Ogden, 2009; Roughgarden, 2004). To achieve more, we must live *beyond* animal instinct— without denying instinct's power! We must find a pathway for learning modern skills—skills that also reflect human instinct.

For humans (and as many as 90 other thus far documented species), sexual relationships are for *more* than mating. Sex is engaged in frequently, with multiple partners, for pleasure. Humans remain the most complex of earth life in terms of brain function. Research reveals as many as 12 brain areas, some seemingly unrelated to sex, "lighting up" during sex and orgasm (Whipple & Komisurak, 2003).

Monogamy Is Not Defined the Same by Everyone

Many a couple have sat before me and declared themselves to be monogamous, even though they have sexual contact with extramarital partners. Studies show that self-identified sexually monogamous couples develop their own definitions and practices (Frank & DeLamater, 2010). Many couples consider themselves monogamous even though they "swing," or share sex with other couples who are friends—a sort of *couple's friends with benefits* arrangement.

Swinging is sometimes considered a monogamous sexual activity because the spouses do it together (as opposed to each of them having sex with separate outside partners). They consider it just another activity of their mutually exclusive sex life.

And then there's cheating. Outside sex with or without love happens in millions of traditionally monogamous relationships. But in traditional monogamy, the price for telling the truth is so high that deception is the rule. Cheating breeds guilt, resentment, and a foundation for much hurt and damage to the relationship and to every person involved.

Monogamy Is Not the Only Workable, Loving Choice

Longitudinal research supports the success of multiple partner adult relationships and their families (Emens, 2004; Orion, 2008a, 2008b, 2011; Sheff, 2014, 2017). Benefits of polyamory, one form of consensual nonmonogamy, include more love and sex, personal growth, deepened communication, expanded families, shared responsibilities and resources. Open marriage arrangements can help maintain intimacy and sexual relations between the married spouses, as well as preventing boredom and stagnation. Otherwise compatible partners who have differing desire levels may stay together and with their children years longer, if outside sex partners are allowed for the more interested spouse (Orion, 2008a, 2008b, 2011).

We now accept that homosexuality is normal for many people, as are heterosexuality and many other choices and sexualities. There is, in short, a range of orientations on a continuum of sexual practices and behaviors. These may or may not match self-identifications. As someone who studies humans, I know that people may use the same terms for different behaviors or feelings, and that individuals may state that they live according to one sexual orientation while not disclosing frequent thoughts and desires associated with another orientation. Stigma also represses many from honest self-reporting.

Socialization makes the customs of any culture "normal" to those in it. Acceptance of the monogamy story, or of the idea of multiple spouses, are cultural mores. Other than polygyny, we have no established cultural models for multiple marriage. Twenty-first-century multiple relationships vary significantly from polygyny, but in a culturally monogamous society, it is easily assumed that anything other than sexual exclusivity means wanton promiscuity or chattel-based, abusive practice. Young men and women may sow wild oats, or have a series of relationships, but eventually will settle down into expected marriage with one spouse.

Can consensual monogamy work at all? In addition to researching polyamory and working with CNM partners, I help many sexually exclusive couples restore, reboot, and recreate intimacy in their relationships. I've seen many happy, long-term monogamous couples who claim they have always been completely monogamous, and some probably have. People are different; some are more suited for a single relationship than are others.

If a couple changes their minds and decides to have extramarital sex, then they are no longer traditionally monogamous. They have joined the growing population practicing consensual nonmonogamy.

References

Buss, D. M. (2017). Strategies of human mating. Plenary presentation at the annual conference of the American Association of Sex Educators, Counselors, and Therapists, Las Vegas, NV, June 16, 2017.

Cloud, J. (1999, November 15). Henry & Mary & Janet & . . . Is your marriage a little dull? The "polyamorists" say there's another way. *Time, 154* (20), 90–91.

Conley, T. D., Moors, A. C., Matsick, J. L., & Ziegler, A. (2013). The fewer the merrier? Assessing stigma surrounding consensually nonmonogamous romantic relationships. *Analyses of Social Issues and Public Policy, 13*, 1–30.

Day, M. V., Kay, A. C., Holmes, J. G., & Napier, J. L. (2011). System justification and the defense of committed relationship ideology. *Journal of Personal and Social Psychology, 101*, 291–306.

DePaulo, B. M., & Morris, W. L. (2005). Singles in society and science. *Psychological Inquiry, 16*, 57–83.

Emens, E. F. (2004). Monogamy's law: Compulsory monogamy and polyamorous existence. *NYU Review of Law & Social Change, 29*, 277–376.

Ferrer, J. N. (2007, January/February). Monogamy, polyamory, and beyond. *Tikkun, 22*, 37–62.

Fisher, H. E. (2016). *Anatomy of love: A natural history of mating, marriage, and why we stray.* (2nd ed.). New York: W.W. Norton.

Frank, K., & DeLamater, J. (2010). Deconstructing monogamy: Boundaries, identities, and fluidities across relationships. In M. Barker, & D. Landridge (Eds.), *Understanding nonmonogamies* (pp. 9–22). New York: Routledge.

Gray, B. P. & Garcia, J. R. (2013). *Evolution and human sexual behavior.* Cambridge, MA: Harvard University Press.

Haupert, M., Gesselman, A., Moors, A., Fisher, H., & Garcia, J. (2016). Prevalence of experiences with consensual non-monogamous relationships: findings from two nationally representative samples of single Americans. *Journal of Sex & Marital Therapy*, doi: 10.1080/0092623X.2016.1178675.

King, B. J. (2017). A cultural moment for polyamory. Retrieved March 23, 2017, from www.npr.org/sections/13.7/2017/03/23/521199308/a-cultural-moment-for-polyamory

Lovemore.com. (2007). Retrieved October 17 from www.lovemore.com/faq.shtm

Mackay, J. (2000). Global sex: Sexuality and sexual practices around the world. Paper presented at Fifth Congress of European Federation of Sexology, Berlin, June 29–July 2 Available at: http://222.2hu-berlin.de/sexology/

Merriam-Webster dictionary. Monogamy. Retrieved August 23, 2016, from www.merriam-webster.com/dictionary/monogamy

Moors, A. C., Matsick, J. L., Ziegler, A., Rubin, J., & Conley, T. D. (2013). Stigma toward individuals engaged in consensual nonmonogamy: Robust and worthy of additional research. *Analysis of Social Issues and Public Policy, 13*, 52–69.

Ogden, G. (2009). Lecture on sexological practice at a meeting of AASECT professionals for continuing education credit, Arlington, MA, May.

Orion, R. (2008a). *From traditional to open marriage.* Case study report. San Francisco: Saybrook Graduate School & Research Center.

Orion, R. (2008b). Polyamory as treatment for low desire. Paper presented at the Western Regional Conference of the Society for the Scientific Study of Sexuality, San Diego, CA, April.

Orion, R. (2011). Examining definitions and treatments of low desire and low-sex marriage (Doctoral dissertation). Available from ProQuest Dissertations and Theses Global database (Dissertation No. 3465923).

Roughgarden, J. (2004). Darwin and gender diversity. Plenary paper presented at Western Regional Conference of the Society for the Scientific Study of Sexuality, San Francisco, May 27.

Sheff, E. A. (2014). *The polyamorists next door: Inside multiple relationships and families.* Lanham, MD: Rowman & Littlefield.

Sheff, E.A. (2017). Personal conversation with author, September 23.

Strong, B., & DeVault, C. (1992). *The marriage and family experience* (5th ed.). St. Paul, MN: West.

Whipple, B., & Komisurak, B. (2003). Brain imaging (FMRI and PET) studies during orgasm in women with and without complete spinal cord injury. Plenary paper presented at Annual Conference of Society for the Scientific Study of Sexuality, San Antonio, TX, May.

2 Social and Clinical Misconceptions about Consensual Nonmonogamy (CNM)

"It is not our differences that divide us. It is our inability to recognize, accept, and celebrate those differences," a truth beautifully stated by Audre Lorde (1994).

Stigma exists. Being openly *polyamorous* or consensually nonmonogamous in any form can literally be dangerous. Additionally, finding safe, informed, and effective clinical help for people in alternative relationship modes is shown as one of the main problems with being outside the accepted norm (Emens, 2004; Haupert, Gesselman, Moors, Fisher, & Garcia, 2016; Henrich & Trawinski, 2016; Orion, 2007, 2008a, 2008b, 2011; Sheff, 2014; Weitzman, 1999, 2006).

Most U.S. therapists are trained to be monocentric—monogamy is the expected norm, making any other relationship type deviant by default. Just as the practice of converting homosexuals was accepted before the 1970s when being gay was finally declared "normal," research shows that many consensual nonmonogamists are told they have to choose between partners if they want help from the therapist (Henrich & Trawinski, 2016; Orion, 2007, 2008a, 2008b). Consensual nonmonogamy (CNM) clients seek clinical help for many of the same reasons anyone else does, as well as for issues unique to responsible multipartnering. When therapists assume that any problem presented by CNM partners exists only because of their alternative relationship, clients are harmed or left unaided and more marginalized.

As presented in a research and literature review report by Haupert et al. (2016), sexuality-based stigma and discrimination can create a hostile social environment and ultimately lead to mental health issues. "People engaged in consensual nonmonogamy experience unjustified stigma, as empirical evidence does not support the belief that these individuals are fundamentally flawed citizens, poor relationship partners, or inadequate parents." As most therapists lack adequate training, clinicians can actually cause or perpetuate client distress (Haupert et al., 2016).

Research by Haupert et al. (2016) and other sources presents estimates that as many as one in five Americans have engaged in some form of consensual nonmonogamy, and that numbers are growing. Making a safe therapeutic space for this population means clinicians must be willing to examine their biases and accept that monogamy as a mainstream norm is prescribed culturally—but is not the only honest, healthy, or successful relationship format. Indeed, observation of western culture reveals that monogamy is unsuccessful at least half the time (Emens, 2004; Mackay, 2000; Orion, 2011; Strong & DeVault, 1992).

Clinicians serving this population need to understand what polyamory and other forms of consensual nonmonogamy are—and also what they are not. It must be accepted by the therapist that CNM is ethical, honest, and scientifically supported as a human norm with lifestyles existing on a continuum. It is necessary for therapists to be clear as to their knowledge of what CNM clients are talking about, and that these clients will not be evaluated with judgment. As with all other clients, CNM clients need to know that they are safe and accepted—even if we, as therapists, are still learning about these new modes and models for relationships and families.

To fully grasp the realities of consensual nonmonogamy, as described in Chapter 3, we must clear the mental and emotional decks of a clutter of misconceptions. Several objections based on misinformation are aimed at polyamory, a major form of consensual nonmonogamy. Polyamorous relationships may consist of multiple partners who live together as spouses or as family; many polyamorous partners have children. Other types of consensual nonmonogamy include swinging and open marriage. Common misconceptions and objections to the various forms of CNM include the following:

- CNM is against all religions.
- CNM is polygyny.
- CNM is illegal.
- CNM is abusive or inappropriate for children.
- CNM is sex addiction.
- CNM signals attachment disorder.
- CNM signals mental health problems.
- CNM demonstrates that partner(s) cannot commit.
- CNM is cheating.
- CNM indicates marriage problems.
- CNM is "just for irresponsible fun."

Let us examine each of these misconceptions.

Is Consensual Nonmonogamy Against All Religions?

Of course, any type of extramarital sex is banned by many religions. Religion sources much of our cultural programming. Indeed, some religions, while accepting sex within marriage as a necessity, seem to frown on enjoying sex. Not all religions are against honest multiple relationships, however.

Unitarian Universalism (UU) is the seventh-largest denomination in the United States and has its roots in European Christianity (www.UUA.org). Within the UU population nationwide are groups working to include into bylaws accept-ance of polyamory and to openly welcome polyamorous partners and families into congregations. As of this writing, the Unitarian Universalist Association has not published a national acceptance policy, but many individual congrega-tions are discussing it and do have polyamorous families as members. A national polyamorous segment of the UUA is active online and in many locations (www.UUPoly.org).

Wasick-Correa (2010) found that among polyamorous research respondents, a variety of religious affiliations were reported. In order of greater to lesser num-bers of participants, these include Pagan, "other," Christian, atheist, Jewish, and Buddhist.

In the sexology field, it is common knowledge that some Eastern-oriented spiritual groups exist who are accepting of honest multipartnering. Eastern tradi-tions teach transformation of jealousy into a sympathetic joy or *mudita*, which is regarded as one of the four immeasurable states or qualities of an enlightened person (Ferrer, 2007). One example is Tantric sexuality or "Tantra," which originated in India and was part of lifestyle, religious beliefs, and practices for 400 years (www.Tantra.com, 2012). The *Kama Sutra*, a publication widely available and recognized in the United States as a source for sexual training, originates from the Tantric tradition of India. Love is not considered finite. Sexuality is considered a skill as well as a sharing of sacred energy, which can be accessed by anyone willing to learn, and which is owned by no one. Tantric training is avail-able in the United States today, and those who espouse any part of this lifestyle or its values may accept and practice honest multipartnering.

Is Consensual Nonmonogamy Polygyny?

Polyamory is a major form of consensual nonmonogamy and is often misun-derstood as *polygyny* (multiple spouses). Polygyny is accepted by many reli-gions worldwide and has been the cultural norm in 70% of nations historically (Strong & DeVault, 1992). Polyamory, however, is not polygyny. There are major differences between polyamory and polygyny.

Polygamy (one husband, multiple wives) is based on wealth or position. Wives are property, sometimes concubines, acquired for the purpose of offspring, who are also considered property. Wives are not allowed to have more than one husband. In some polygamous cultures, girls barely reaching puberty are married off. Children and even babies are often promised as chattel in marriage agreements to be carried out later (also common among royalty in monogamous cultures).

About 1% of cultures historically, worldwide, practice *polyandry*, which allows or forces women to have multiple male partners (Strong & Devault, 1992). Polyamory is neither sexist nor chattel-based. Polyamory is love-based and egali-tarian; both men and women have equal rights to be with additional partners.

Polyamory does not involve children in adult practices. While many polyam-orous partners are parents, the sexual relations between adults does not alter the responsible care of children. Just as monogamous couples keep adult activities appropriately away from their children, so do polyamorous parents. Just as gay and lesbian couples are responsible and healthy parents, so are polyamorous adults—whether or not this is currently recognized in the mainstream. Longitudinal research shows that children are not more at risk in poly families (Anapol, 2010; Orion, 2008a, 2008b; Sheff, 2014; Sheff, 2017).

Is Consensual Nonmonogamy Illegal?

Consensual nonmonogamy is not illegal. Polyamory is not bigamy. CNM relationships do not necessarily include marriage. Some polyamorous partner groups may include one legally married couple. Some partners may create personal commitment ceremonies—spiritual marriages with a union ritual—with more than one partner. Legal papers can be drawn up to cover adults and children in the family who are not protected by laws and benefits of legal marriage. None of these activities is against the law.

Is Consensual Nonmonogamy Abusive or Inappropriate for Children?

We once did not accept that two parents of the same sex could appropriately and successfully raise happy, healthy children. We now understand differently. Research also shows that polyamorous relationships, including those with children in the house, last just as short—or long—as do monogamous relationships with children (Anapol, 2010; Orion, 2008a, 2008b, 2011; Sheff, 2014, 2017).

The capacity to be honest and loving with more than one adult suggests more loving and responsible caregivers, rather than any tendency for abuse or irresponsibility to children. The values of polyamory are about love and respect for everyone; this does not breed abusive behavior toward children. I have worked with hundreds of people who are in some way living a CNM lifestyle and many of them are parents; my professional experience supports these ideas. I have seen less bad parenting among polyamorous than monogamous clients. The fact that there are more unrelated adults in a poly household may mitigate against abuse.

It is well known that children can benefit from varied role models. Most modern parents are very busy and may not be perfect models for children. To the extent that more people than a child's parents are directly involved with childcare may be a good thing. The average American nuclear family is under stress, often with two working parents. The extended family has historically been a factor in rearing healthy children and running busy households. Many poly partners are considered immediate or extended family members and play an equally important role (Anapol, 2010; Barker, n.d.; Orion, 2008a, 2011; Sheff, 2014, 2017). It is also true that relations, in-laws, and extended family members can be toxic in any particular family constellation.

Is Consensual Nonmonogamy Sex Addiction?

"Sex addiction" is itself an unsound and faulty term, certainly not an accurate nor accepted diagnosis. There are books on the topic of so-called sex addiction; this is not one of them. I state only that the *Diagnostic and Statistical Manual V* (APA, 2013) rejected the use of the term "sex addiction" as a diagnosis. In the professional sexology field, the concept and definition of addiction with regard to sex are also not accepted. The American Association of Sex Educators, Counselors, and Therapists (www.AASECT.org), founded in 1967 to promote sexual health and the advancement of sex education and therapy, issued a statement in 2016 that the diagnosis of sex addiction is faulty and not accepted by the organization. AASECT is internationally recognized as providing scientifically based and academically sound training and documentation for sex educators, counselors, and therapists:

> AASECT recognizes that people may experience significant physical, psychological, spiritual, and sexual health consequences related to their sexual urges, thoughts, or behaviors. AASECT recommends that its members utilize models that do not unduly pathologize consensual sexual problems. AASECT 1) does not find sufficient empirical evidence to support the classification of sex addiction or porn addiction as a mental health disorder, and 2) does not find the sexual addiction training and treatment methods and educational pedagogies to be adequately informed by accurate human sexuality knowledge. Therefore it is the position of AASECT that linking problems related to sexual urges, thoughts, or behaviors to a porn/sexual addiction process cannot be advanced by AASECT as a standard practice for sexuality education delivery, counseling, or therapy. AASECT advocates for a collaborative movement to establish standards of care supported by science, public health consensus, and the rigorous protection of sexual rights for consumers seeking treatments for problems related to consensual sexual urges, thoughts, or behaviors.

People can develop risky, unhealthy, and compulsive behaviors involving sex (or food, or playing games). The current term in professional sexology for these behaviors is *out of control sexual behavior* or OCSB (Braun-Harvey, 2017). Scientifically, there is no norm for how much sex is "too much." We have no empirically determined "normal" amount of sex to want or have (Orion, 2011).

Are some in CNM lifestyles compulsively acting out unresolved issues in multiple relationships? Possibly. Many who are not in CNM relationships are sexually compulsive, dishonest, and unsafe. Multiple relationships are complicated. CNM is not an easy way to have compulsive sex. CNM requirements include honesty, safe practices, and a lot of communication, all of which inhibit compulsivity. A client displaying risky or compulsive sexual behaviors may have OCSB (which may require sex therapy training to determine). Such a client needs help, regardless of the format or number of relationships involved.

In extrapolating from the literature, which shows few differences in certain problems between CNM and monogamy, I believe it is likely that there are no more sexually compulsive people in CNM than otherwise, and probably fewer. To the extent that a lot of sexual activity may exist, CNM folks are honest about it.

Does Consensual Nonmonogamy Signal Attachment Disorder?

It has been my experience that because training in sexuality and alternative relationships is unavailable, some therapists diagnose CNM clients as having attachment disorder. Attachment disorder is often characterized by an inability to form intimate attachments. Some research (Morrison et al., 2013) shows that polyamorous men and women manifest greater levels of intimacy than monogamous study participants. Other research (Moors, Conley, Edelstein, & Chopik, 2015) reveals that avoidant individuals are less likely to engage in polyamorous relationships despite positive attitudes about consensual nonmonogamy. Ramirez and Brown (2010) found no significant difference in attachment styles between open and closed relationships of gay men.

We can infer that there are no more incidents of attachment problems in CNM relationships than in any other relationship format; there even may be fewer. People bring their problems into relationships, regardless of how many partners they have. CNM situations do not cause any individual's attachment problems. People do not choose CNM because of attachment problems, and those with such problems may avoid multiple partnerships.

Does Consensual Nonmonogamy Signal Mental Health Problems?

That those in CNM relationships are *neurotic, unsatisfied, or otherwise mentally ill* are beliefs held even among psychological experts (Rubel & Bogaert, 2015). Studies show that to the extent persons in CNM have more distress than those in monogamous relationships, these stressors are more due to the stigma and danger that CNM potentially presents: judgment from and loss of acceptance by family members and friends; possible loss of employment; the necessity of hiding one's true self and relationships (Rubel & Bogaert, 2015). Books and reports by CNM practitioners, and more studies than can be listed, document that persons who are polyamorous, who practice swinging, or who live in open relationships must develop good relationship skills, develop higher self-esteem, and undergo personal examination and growth.

People in CNM lifeways are not automatically healthier or more skilled than everyone else. Making a success of CNM requires learning and growth, as well as courage to live against the mainstream and to share one's intimate partner(s). These are not signs of poor mental health.

Does Consensual Nonmonogamy Demonstrate that Partners Cannot Commit?

A deep and complicated commitment is required to enter into honest consensual nonmonogamy. Every partner is a real person with feelings, schedules, responsibilities—a life. CNM multiplies this: more to be responsible about because of more individuals. There are more issues and time demands to deal with, even if it is a swinging situation with less ongoing relationship depth and involvement. The word *consensual* means those enlisted have to discuss and come to agreements as to what they are consenting to.

Someone who has difficulty with commitment in general will probably have the same difficulty in any type or number of relationships. On the other hand, I have had clients who had difficulty with monogamy but are extremely committed and responsible in CNM because CNM reflects who they are, and because they learn about love and gain skills that are not required in monogamy.

Is Consensual Nonmonogamy Cheating?

Our culture has no models for honest multipartnering. The average nonmonogamous individual may have many relationships that are not well handled, or may enter a monogamous commitment, with genuine sincerity. Compelled by any number of factors into additional relations, there is no accepted cultural option to discuss this, nor to create an expansion to the monogamous relationship. The cheating partner understandably fears telling the truth, which has very high costs—shame, fear of hurting loved ones, possible loss of partner, friends, and family. The illicit affair may bring unwanted health issues into the picture. The essence of cheating is a lack of understanding about human sexuality, followed by deceit and nonnegotiated betrayal of relationship commitment.

A study on attitudes toward nonexclusive relationships concludes that the aspect which has most effect on judgment is whether or not the structure of the relationship has been agreed upon by all parties (Grunt-Mejer & Campbell, 2015). In a CNM situation, nonmonogamous individuals are accepted, and they have guidelines on behaving with integrity in each relationship. CNM is the opposite of cheating—every person knows about each relationship, and all partners negotiate how commitments will be carried out, or changed. Many studies and reported sexological clinical experience show that CNM engenders better safe sex practices (see Chapter 9) and deeper, more consistent communication.

Does Consensual Nonmonogamy Indicate Marriage Problems?

Reports from clients and in the field of sexology reveal that therapists may not believe CNM clients are actually comfortable with their situation. A primary couple comes for help with any number of issues; if they are honest and tell the therapist about other partners, the therapist may be taken aback. Deep feelings and attitudes, supported by mainstream monogamy-centric training, cause reactions the therapist cannot hide (Henrich & Trawinski, 2016). If the therapist has had personal experience of being cheated on, or grew up in a household with such problems, countertransference may occur.

CNM clients have reported to me that they had to either educate another therapist about consensual nonmonogamy, and got little assistance with their presenting concerns, or that they had to leave that therapist because the therapist would not work with them unless they "gave up the affair." I have heard many reports from clients that non-CNM-aware therapists viewed the open relationship as a serious problem with their marriage. That anyone could genuinely love, and honestly carry out, a relationship with more than one person—or agree to their partners doing so—was simply too foreign a concept and must be pathological.

Clinicians must examine their deeply held beliefs, their personal experiences, and question their training with regard to monogamy, to get on the current science train. CNM is not for everyone but is as potentially healthy, workable, honest, and safe a relationship and family lifeway as is monogamy; it is as successful and long term, or not, as is monogamy (Anapol, 2010; Orion 2008a, 2008b, 2011; Sheff, 2014, 2017). There are too many other sources to present all.

If a therapist wants to serve this population, it is the ethical duty of the clinician to examine him/herself and to expand diversity training to work with this alternative and rapidly growing population, with compassion and knowledge.

Is Consensual Nonmonogamy "Just for Irresponsible Fun"?

Those who think CNM is fun and try this mode of living soon find out instead how difficult consensual nonmonogamy can be. Many in polyamorous relationships and families state that they were compelled into the situation, that it was not a choice for fun, and that sex is not the top reason why they are polyamorous (Orion, 2007, 2008a, 2011). An expanded monogamy such as swinging may be more of a choice for fun, variety, and excitement, but practitioners still find that it is not all fun and games. There are health and safety concerns, issues of time, disclosure, discretion, and respect for all partners, no matter how casual the relationship situation.

Being sex positive, I also state that there is nothing wrong with having fun sex! Various forms of morality may dictate otherwise, but scientifically, as a sexologist in the field for 17 years, and with decades of scientific sexual research behind us, which has not since been refuted, humans by nature seek, enjoy, and benefit from sex, whether or not it is within a committed relationship. It is OK if sex helps us feel better. It is OK if there are a variety of partners, as long as these are consenting adults who practice sex safety. It is OK if sex is "just for fun." This is not all that humans need in the way of relating or sexuality, but sexual fun is healthy and helpful if carried out responsibly. Responsibility means safety for one's self and partners, physically and emotionally. That includes consent, with adults only.

As stated by Dr. Christiane Northrop (2015) and backed by much research in several fields, "pleasure isn't just for fun—it's necessary for our health." So are skin and body contact; these are inherent in sexual activities, although usually not thought of as part of what we are seeking. We may become aware of the needs of body and skin contact if we lose sex from our life.

Managing relationships and sexual behavior safely and with integrity is important. Love and sex, perhaps even with variety and frequency, are natural to health, survival, adaptation, and happiness. Stephen Harrod Buhner writes in his research-based book, *Plant Intelligence and the Imaginal Realm*, that sex is woven into the fabric of Earth, into us, and the world:

> [S]ex really is fundamental to system functioning. Unsurprisingly, frequent sex stimulates the formation of new neurons in neural networks, irrespective of the type or age of the organism. Sensory gating channels open more widely, cognition improves, functionality increases, homeodynamics improves.
>
> (2014, p. 161)

What used to be considered hippie ideas of open love and sex are now backed by many fields of science. "Love the one you're with" has continued to be part of social evolution, a modern adaptation of true human nature. Consensual nonmonogamy is a blueprint for loving as many as we may be with, responsibly.

Conclusion

Unfortunately many individuals contribute to the pool of those who are not responsible, cannot commit, have attachment disorders, are abusive, are poor parents, cheat, are terrible spouses, and display multiple risky and compulsive behaviors, sexually and otherwise. Regardless of the number or type of partners in a relationship, individuals come complete with their problems. Not all CNM relationships are successful, but within CNM, partners likely work to be responsible because more people are concerned about all behaviors; there are more persons to discuss problems and to insist on finding and carrying out resolutions.

References

AASECT (American Association of Sex Educators, Counselors, and Therapists). (2016). *AASECT position on sex addiction*. Available at: www.aasect.org/position-sex-addiction

Anapol, D. (2010). *Polyamory in the 21st century: Love and intimacy with multiple partners*. Lanham, MD: Rowman & Littlefield.

APA (American Psychiatric Association). (2013). *Diagnostic and statistical manual of mental disorders* (5th ed.). Washington, DC: American Psychiatric Association.

Barker, M. (n.d.). *This is my partner and this is my partner's partner: Constructing a polyamorous identity in a monogamous world*. Enfield, Middlesex, UK: Middlesex University.

Braun-Harvey, D. (2017). What is healthy sexuality? Plenary presentation. Annual Conference of the American Association of Sex Educators, Counselors, and Therapists. Las Vegas, NV, June.

Buhner, S. H. (2014). *Plant intelligence and the imaginal realm* (pp. 160–161). Rochester, VT: Bear & Company.

Emens, E. F. (2004). Monogamy's law: Compulsory monogamy and polyamorous existence. *NYU Review of Law & Social Change, 29,* 277–327.

Ferrer, J. N. (2007, January/February). Monogamy, polyamory, and beyond. *Tikkun, 22,* 37–62.

Grunt-Mejer, K., & Campbell, C. (2015). Around consensual nonmonogamies: Assessing attitudes toward nonexclusive relationships. *The Journal of Sex Research, 53* (1): 45–53.

Haupert, M., Gesselman, A., Moors, A., Fisher, H., & Garcia, J. (2016). Prevalence of experiences with consensual non-monogamous relationships: Findings from two nationally representative samples of single Americans. *Journal of Sex & Marital Therapy,* doi: 10.1080/0092623X.2016.1178675.

Henrich, R., & Trawinski, C. (2016). Social and relationship challenges facing polyamorous clients. *Sexual and Relationship Therapy.* Available at: http:/dx.doi.org/10.1080/148681994.2016.117.4331

Lorde, A. (1994). *Our dead behind us: Poems.* New York: W.W. Norton & Co.

Mackay, J. (2000). Global sex: Sexuality and sexual practices around the world. Paper presented at Fifth Congress of European Federation of Sexology, Berlin, June 29–July 2. Available at: http://222.2hu-berlin.de/sexology/

Moors, A., Conley, T., Edelstein, R., & Chopik, W. (2015). Attached to monogamy? Avoidance predicts willingness to engage (but not actual engagement) in consensual nonmonogamy. *Journal of Social and Personal Relationships, 32* (2), 222–240.

Morrison, T., Beaulieu, D., Brockman, M., & Beaglaoich, C. (2013). A comparison of polyamorous and monoamorous persons: Are there differences in indices of relationship well-being and sociosexuality? *Psychology & Sexuality, 4,* 75–91.

Northrop, C. (2015). Women's bodies, women's wisdom. *PBS presentation by Christiane Northrop,* September.

Orion, R. (2007). *Polyamory and the bisexual marriage.* Research report. San Francisco: Saybrook Graduate School and Research Center.

Orion, R. (2008a). *From traditional to open marriage.* Case study report. San Francisco: Saybrook Graduate School & Research Center.

Orion, R. (2008b). Polyamory as treatment for low desire. Paper presented at the Western Regional Conference of the Society for the Scientific Study of Sexuality, San Diego, CA, April.

Orion, R. (2011). Examining definitions and treatments of low desire and low-sex marriage (Doctoral dissertation). Available from ProQuest Dissertations and Theses Global database (Dissertation No. 3465923).

Ramirez, O. M., & Brown, J. (2010). Attachment style, rules regarding sex, and couple satisfaction: A study of gay male couples. *Australian and New Zealand Journal of Family Therapy, 31* (2), 202–213.

Rubel, A., & Bogaert, A. (2015). Consensual nonmonogamy: Psychological well-being and relationship quality correlates. *The Journal of Sex Research, 52* (9), 961–982, doi: 10.1080/00224499.2014.942722.

Sheff, E. A. (2014). *The polyamorists next door: Inside multiple relationships and families.* Lanham, MD: Rowman & Littlefield.

Sheff, E. A. (2017). Personal interview with author, September 23.

Strong, B. & DeVault, C. (1992). *The marriage and family experience* (5th ed.). St. Paul, MN: West.

Wasick-Correa, K. (2010). Agreements, rules and agentic fidelity in polyamorous relationships. *Psychology and Sexuality*, *1*, 1. Available at: http:/dx.doi.org/10.1080/19419891003634471

Weitzman, G. D. (1999). What psychology professionals should know about polyamory: The lifestyles and mental health concerns of polyamorous individuals. Paper presented at 8th Annual Diversity Conference, Albany, NY, March.

Weitzman, G. D. (2006). Therapy with clients who are bisexual and polyamorous. *Journal of Bisexuality*, *6* (1–2), 137–164. doi: 10.1300/J159v06n01_08.

www.Tantra.com. A website no longer active after several years of offering history and other information on Tantric traditions, spiritual, and sexual training for the westerner. Accessed 2012.

www.UUPoly.org. Active website of Unitarian Universalists for polyamory awareness.

3 Understanding Consensual Nonmonogamy

Consensual nonmonogamy (CNM), also known as responsible multipartnering, exists when partners have decided together to allow—and to be honest about—having more than one sexual relationship at the same time. Consensus and honesty are the hallmarks of CNM.

According to the Merriam-Webster dictionary, "consensual" is defined as:

(1) Existing or made by mutual *consent* [to give assent or approval: agree: to be in concord in opinion or sentiment] without an act of writing; *a consensual contract*.
(2) Involving or based on mutual consent; *consensual acts*.

"Polyamory" refers to loving more than one person simultaneously, including sexually, in significant ongoing relationships. Single individuals who espouse the values of polyamory may be considered polyamorous.

"Expanded monogamy" is a term I use to describe married or committed couples who expand their sex lives. These may include swingers who don't look for love relationships, couples who share sexual encounters with friends, and couples who allow extramarital relationships but do not share partners. The formats include open relationships and swinging.

Expanded monogamy includes two types of relationships:

- *Swinging*: Often with short-term or anonymous partners; love relationships are neither sought nor intended; couples may consider themselves monogamous because they share the outside sex together.
- *Open relationship*: A relationship that is open to additional partners who may not identify with polyamory or swinging. Both partners may not choose to seek ongoing additional relationships. Either may or may not know their partner's other partners. Single individuals who espouse open sexual values may belong to this group.

Haupert, Gesselman, Moors, Fisher, and Garcia (2016) describe CNM as including three subtypes: (1) *polyamory* (romantic, loving, and long term in nature); (2) *swinging* (sexual in nature); and (3) *open relationships* (primarily sexual in nature but can also be romantic).

Regardless of how CNM is defined or by whom, every type of consensual nonmonogamy must adhere to these rules to be successful:

- CNM requires honesty.
- CNM exists on a continuum.
- CNM is hard work.
- CNM has reported benefits.
- CNM exists in various formats.

Consensual Nonmonogamy Requires Honesty

By definition, CNM means that all partners know that other partners are involved. Each individual makes an informed decision to be intimate, even if indirectly, with more than one other. This *consensus* creates the necessary context for every partner to incorporate health, safety, and emotional responsibility with each other partner.

How and what is revealed by partners may not be perfect, but *consensual* nonmonogamy is being practiced only when every person involved is aware of all others involved.

Consensual Nonmonogamy Exists on a Continuum

As Kinsey (1948) discovered, all kinds of people do all kinds of things. Kinsey developed a scale of sexual orientation: heterosexual to homosexual with variations in between. This helped individuals identify themselves among groups of newly accepted norms. Where a person is on that scale may reflect lifestyles and attitudes as well as sexual orientation. While Kinsey's scale may not represent the additions and complexities of today's world of sexual and gender orientation, the model of a scale or continuum is useful in understanding consensual nonmonogamy.

Labels and what they mean are not important to some but are very important to others. Marginalized individuals are helped by finding out they belong with others who are similar and sympathetic. While there is some agreement as to the meanings of commonly used CNM terms, individuals, couples, triads, quads, or pods may have developed definitions of their own. Therapists need to understand what labels mean to those who use them. If partners do not use terms, it may be helpful to define or create some. To learn about and identify with a particular label may clarify a place along the continuum of belonging. In therapy, it is important to have each person describe what is meant by the terms used. This builds a framework for illuminating each person's expectations, and her or his roles and partnerships in the group. Whether or not labels are used by CNM clients, the therapist needs to discover each person's expectations, visions, and ideas.

The continuum of consensual nonmonogamy is on one end, close to tradition; on the other are radical new models. Variations exist in between. The major differences between one end of the CNM continuum and the other are attitudes, behaviors, and levels of involvement. Partners who view themselves as being in a traditional relationship live as committed couples, but have some form of open or expanded sexual agreement. Such partners may or may not seek ongoing meaningful additional partners; shared information and experiences vary in amount and depth. The most traditional are *don't ask, don't tell* couples. They have a negotiated open agreement, but neither one knows the other's outside partners, and the couple does not share information or logistics of their extramarital (or relationship) partners. In other words, this couple made an agreement, but they rarely if ever talk about it, and they share nothing of each other's outside activities. They are, however, honest about their marriage with outside partners.

On the other end of the continuum are partners who are living radically new lifestyles. This includes those who find themselves in (or seek and want) meaningful, ongoing love relationships with all partners, whether or not all partners live together, and regardless of how time is shared. Representing the most inclusive polyamory might be a poly family with three or more adult partners, all of whom live together and share intimacy as well as finances, parenting, and household management.

In between these extremes are open couples who do share knowledge of extra partners; those who have meaningful relationships with extramarital partners who do not live in; swingers who are married or committed and share their sexual liaisons with partners; couples who share sex with friends they care about, but not with in-love relationships. All relationship types of CNM include consent and honesty, but why and how relationships are carried out takes many forms.

For many who practice CNM, it can be considered a lifestyle, engaged in for social and *sexual variety*, a positive psychological adaptation for humans (Buss, 2017). For others, research has referred to polyamory as not only a lifestyle but an identity, which emerges "as the fluid expression of experience that is the . . . result of environment, social context, inner states, and personal history" (Henrich & Trawinski, 2016).

CNM Is Hard Work

Those observers referred to as the "poly curious" think the idea of being allowed to have sex with more people must be fun. Those who practice CNM say it can be fun, but overall a lot of work is involved in carrying out responsibly more than one intimate relationship at a time. "Poly" people and others in expanded monogamy are individual humans—no more automatically gifted in successful relationships than anyone else. Those in CNM find themselves compelled by genuinely loving more than one person, or they are oriented toward a more open, varietal sex life than monogamy provides; in either case they choose to live and love honestly.

Success with any form of consensual nonmonogamy may include the necessity of getting professional help with these relationship requirements:

- personal growth;
- communication skills;
- placing more value on love and freedom than on jealousy;
- managing jealousy;
- developing and maintaining boundaries and "rules";
- maintaining family commitments;
- good time management;
- good self-esteem;
- respect for each partner;
- other factors idiosyncratically.

Those who achieve successful CNM relationships deserve all the fun they can get, given the work involved!

Consensual Nonmonogamy Has Reported Benefits

Many sources report that consensual nonmonogamy in all forms has benefits. These include greater (in comparison to infidelity) protection from sexually transmitted infections (Conley, Moors, Ziegler, & Karathanasis, 2012); increased happiness and health among older adults (Fleckenstein & Cox, 2015); increased passion and sexual variety in relationships (Nichols, 2004; Orion, 2008a, 2011); shared parenting and familial responsibilities (Orion, 2008a, 2008b, 2011; Sheff, 2014, 2017). Many sources and my experience show additional benefits including personal and spiritual growth; expanded intimacy and bonding in adult relationships; less pressure in those relationships on the more traditional end of the spectrum; freedom of self-expression; and greater life opportunities for individuals than for some in monogamous relationships. CNM may also support the long-term stability of low-sex couples and their families (Orion, 2008a, 2008b, 2011).

Consensual Nonmonogamy Exists in Various Formats

Polyamory for individuals
Polyamory for couples
Triads and quads
Pods and polycules
Polyhierarchy
Open relationships
Swinging

Polyamory

While many have heard or used the term *polyamory*, not all people who practice consensual nonmonogamy are polyamorous. "Poly" is sometimes used as a catch-all label for any form of CNM, but that is incorrect. *Polyamory* is a word created by Morning Glory Zell in her 1990 article, "A bouquet of lovers." The word translates to "many loves" and was needed to replace the more awkward expression "responsible nonmonogamy" being used by a continuously growing number of people. Cyberspace conversations via the internet and the World Wide Web popularized usage of the new term around the world and helped bring it into general use (Anapol, 1997). This term is now so accepted that the word *polyamory* is in the dictionary. According to the Merriam-Webster dictionary, "polyamory" is defined as: "state or practice of having more than one open romantic relationship at a time."

The word polyamory is recognized and used by millions of people. In my experience, some people use the term "poly" or "polyamory" for every kind of sexually open relationship. Others are clear on the intended meaning and the differences between poly and other forms of CNM. Some folks don't care about terms and may not call themselves anything, though they clearly live a CNM lifestyle.

According to some, polyamory is not only the practice of, but the desire for, maintaining multiple intimate, significant relationships at the same time. These relationships include many elements such as friendship, love, commitment, flirting, romance, and spiritual connection. A research and literature review by Henrich and Trawinski (2016) states that among the range of consensually nonmonogamous relationships, polyamory emphasizes love and emotional intimacy more than the sexual variety underlying some CNM lifestyles. These researchers define polyamory as "an honest and transparent agreement among partners to love more than one person" (p. 2).

According to Anapol (1997), one of the first authoritative writers on polyamory, polyamory is "a lovestyle which arises from the understanding that love cannot be forced to flow, or not flow, in any particular direction" (p. 179). This is an extremely important concept to recognize. Love cannot be forced. Nor can people force themselves to stop loving someone. The basis of polyamory is the acceptance of that fact. Rather than forcing partners to choose between two or more people they have come to love, polyamory is working together to allow love relationships to coexist honestly and with respect for all persons involved. How much of daily life is shared by all parties, and who shares intimacy with whom, are variables depending on situations and individual needs, wants, and capabilities.

The lifeway of polyamory questions the idea of one partner for the rest of one's life being all things to the other partner—career person, friend, co-parent, living companion, family member, and ongoing lover—often an unreasonable and unrealistic expectation. Instead this lifeway demonstrates that people can genuinely and honestly love, and care deeply about, more than one person at a time. This very assertion was published in a popular book of the 1970s, *Open Marriage* by O'Neill and O'Neill, one of the first to bring the idea of CNM to the general public.

These ideas are in grave conflict with much of our social programming, which teaches us that love is finite, and that loving a second person romantically takes love away from the first partner. Observation of humans (science) and the experience of millions (nature) tell us this is not true. Love is an infinite energy. The capacity to receive and to give love is individual and can be developed (unless early damage is severe), but love cannot be either summoned or denied at will. Every relationship is unique. Partners are neither interchangeable nor replaceable any more than are children of a family. Time has to be shared, and compromises made; jealousies do occur. Humans can, however, genuinely love and responsibly care about more than one partner, just as parents care about more than one child.

Polyamory for Individuals

Individuals can be polyamorous even if they are not in a relationship. Research supports the ideas that one can *be* nonmonogamous, as an orientation, and that such orientation can manifest not only as being sexually active with various partners, but as a need for more than one simultaneous love or sexual relationship (Ferrer, 2007; Klesse, 2014; Orion, 2008a, 2011; Tweedy, 2011). Being polyamorous is also a type of personal identity and a lifestyle (Henrich & Trawinski, 2016). Polyamorous individuals may be seeking compatible partners. They may like living alone, or not having a primary partner, but instead have a network of lovers and friends, all of whom are informed of the existence of the others.

Polyamory for Couples

A couple can be polyamorous whether or not they have additional partners. Some couples seek a third significant partner; two couples can share meaningful relationships; both partners of a primary couple may have additional ongoing loves.

Triads and Quads

When three partners share in-depth relationships, or when a couple adds a third partner who is significant to either one of them, they may refer to themselves as a *triad* or *throuple*. A *quad* or *fourple* is four people who, in some combination, share significant relationships, at least some of which include sex.

Mark, Lena, and Carlos are an example of a triad. Mark and Lena are married. Mark is bisexual and fell in love with Carlos. Then Lena also fell in love with Carlos. They decided to all stay together. They refer to themselves as a throuple that is "polyfidelitous," meaning they are sexually exclusive with each other.

Pods and Polycules

Pod and *polycule* are terms sometimes used to describe families with more than two adult partners, groups, communities, or networks of people whose values include honest openness for sexual play together. Pods may be named after whales, who live, love, and play together in groups, even though not all in the group partner or share dwellings. All human pod or polycule partners may not have deep or meaningful relationships, but in theory all share the values of honesty and sexual freedom with responsibility. Pods and polycules may include families, groups, or networks of partners.

Polyhierarchy

Polyhierarchy is a way of organizing multiple roles and relationships. Hierarchies can involve any number of people, not all of whom have to be intimately involved. A triad, for example, may consist of a married couple who view themselves as primary, and a partner who is a "second" to either or both spouses.

The term *primary* usually means that one relationship in a group of three or more individuals is of first importance. That importance may include commitment into the future, children, shared home and finances, and time scheduling. The primary partnership overrides in some aspects, other relationships and interests.

Seconds (and *thirds*, and so on) are additional partner(s) to the primary couple who may or may not live with them. A second is usually a lover and companion of at least one primary partner. The second relationship has ongoing meaning and various degrees of daily life involvement. There may be less shared time allotted to second and additional partners. Certain aspects of roles and arrangements of the secondary partner(s) are considered less primary in practical matters, although not necessarily less *emotionally* important.

Many poly people do not like the hierarchy principle. Some find using a hierarchy model helpful in clarifying each partner's role and limitations in the overall arrangement. Others object to limitations on any of the relationships in the group that are not shared by all.

Open Relationships

The term "open marriage" was made popular by the O'Neill book of the same name in 1973. Couples maintain their traditional marriage and lifestyle in ways other than sex, but allow one another to have extramarital sexual partners. There is variation in how much each partner knows about the other one's additional liaisons. In some open relationships partners share a lot, including discussion of any outside partner before they engage with that person. Others have a *don't ask, don't tell* agreement: Each partner has the right to outside relations, but neither wants to know with whom, where, or when. General rules may be in place, such as not seeing anyone from the town the couple lives in; family plans and commitments must come first and remain intact; health and safety rules must be followed.

Jill and Jack illustrate this variation on the expanded monogamy theme. They are traditionally married. Jill has no interest in sex but agrees that Jack has a right to a sex life. They created a don't ask, don't tell agreement. Jill doesn't want to know who or when Jack dates, but the couple have parameters that protect family time, privacy, and health.

Some open couples seek and share partners together. In an earlier era, this may have been called wife swapping. This can be referred to as *couple friends with benefits*, when the partners who exchange on sex dates are friends in other parts of life.

Denise and Kevin illustrate this variation. Denise and Kevin consider themselves a married couple in the traditional sense, but they share a flexible sexual agreement. This sharing is carried out only with friends whom they both agree are compatible, reliable, and discreet. Their partners are thus friends they know well, so they all feel safe and comfortable, but they are not in love nor living like family with these friends.

Research also reveals a significant number of traditional marriages between one straight and one bisexual spouse (McLean, 2004; Orion, 2007). An open sexual agreement is one way some such marriages survive. Not all bisexual spouses seek relations with both sexes simultaneously; just because a bisexual person is married to a spouse of one sex or the other doesn't mean that she or he must also have a sexual partner of the other sex. I have also worked with bisexual persons who were married to a spouse of one sex for years, then got divorced and married a person of the other sex.

There are situations, however, where a bisexual spouse does need sexual contact with a partner of each gender (Haupert, et al., 2016; Orion, 2007). In these cases, practicing some form of CNM is necessary to respect the bisexual person. Sometimes this is difficult for the straight partner, whose orientation also deserves respect. This is one of the challenges faced in CNM for which therapists need to be prepared.

Swinging

Swinging is generally considered an activity which provides variety and can help a couple maintain sexual excitement and interest. Outside partners may be shared by the primary couple, but these outside partners are not ongoing, romantic, or in-depth relationships:

> They don't mean anything to us, and we don't mean anything to them. It's just to keep variety and excitement in our own sex life. We [spouses] are together when we do it, this is something we share, it's part of our sex life.
>
> (CNM therapy client)

Versions of that explanation have been said in my office many times. While some may consider themselves sexually exclusive but in practice are not, the difference is honesty.

There are swinging clubs and conventions in which participants can have totally anonymous sex in a patrolled environment (bouncer-type employees maintain general safety and following of rules). Some such clubs and groups exist in unexpected places and in geographic areas considered conservative. I've been surprised to learn of many clients who attend sex clubs.

Some who identify as swingers say that they want more than anonymity with their sex dates. They are not seeking ongoing love relationships in daily life, but the stories I've heard in my office reveal that if a good set of swinging partners is found, they may be "keepers." In theory, swingers seek safety, compatibility, reliability, and discretion. Partners with whom to swap sex, who also have these attributes, are not easy to find.

One type of swinging is illustrated by the case of Sanjay and Anita, who interview, then have dinner, with couples they locate online. If they each like the other couple well enough, the foursome exchange partners for evenings of hoped-for fun sex. They may or may not see the same couple again. While this might sound fun or uncomplicated to some people, it can be fraught with dangers and challenges.

I see a lot of gray areas, crossovers, situations starting out anonymous but becoming more involved, and other variations. Some people use terms and labels and feel strongly about how such labels are defined and used. Others don't categorize themselves. Anyone practicing CNM in any form has to figure out how to work out the arrangement they *think* they want, whatever they may call it. Therapists need to be prepared to help clarify these issues.

Popular CNM Vocabulary

In addition to words used as labels for numbers of partners in a relationship (second, triad, and so on), there are terms used as relationship descriptors and for experiences within CNM. Clinicians may find familiarity with some of these terms useful.

Agentic fidelity: Agentic fidelity is described thus by Wasick-Correa (2010):

> By underscoring their ability for multiple loves, there remains a continued emphasis on emotional rather than sexual intimacy . . . agentic fidelity is a certain form of commitment among polyamorists that relies upon acute self-knowledge and choice, exercised through the ability to express needs and boundaries.

Compersion: Often considered the opposite of jealousy, compersion is genuine happiness for a partner's positive experience with and love for another partner. Compared with the feeling of being truly happy for another's good fortune or achievement, compersion is discussed further in Chapter 5 on jealousy.

Monogamish: Some use monogamish as a general term meaning an agreed upon sexual openness or flexibility. Usually this level of openness is not as comprehensive as polyamory, but describes expanded monogamy.

Nesting partner: A live-in partner, who may also be a co-parent, may be called a nesting partner.

New relationship energy (NRE): A phenomenon noted in CNM circles is the excitement and draw for togetherness with a new partner. New relationship energy exists in monogamy, too, but it may be called falling in love, or likened to the early passion of a relationship. NRE is noted among CNM partners as a phase of new relationships which may be intense, but which may calm down when the new partner becomes integrated and the novelty wanes.

Pod: Pod may refer to a group or family consisting of adult partners, or a network of adult partners.

Polycule: Polycule is a term for a family with polyamorous adult partners.

Polyfidelity: Polyfidelity means that all partners within a group are sexual only with each other.

Satellites: Other partners of an individual or of primary partners.

V-formation: V-formation is a term for a configuration within a triad. One woman has two male partners, for example, and the two men are friends but are not romantic or sexual together. The trio spends time together as a triad: They all do things together. The two partner-friends also spend time together, and each of them has private time with the woman. They may or may not live together. There may or may not be a married or central couple involved. The term may indicate equal time, commitment, and involvement with each partner-friend, an alternative to a hierarchical format.

Other shapes of relationship formats may exist with descriptive terms that I have not yet heard and that are not included here. Therapists continue to learn from CNM clients, and research is expanding.

References

Anapol, D. (1997). *Polyamory, the new love without limits: Secrets of sustainable intimate relationships.* San Rafael, CA: IntiNet Resource Center.

Buss, D. M. (2017). Strategies of human mating. Plenary presentation at the annual conference of the American Association of Sex Educators, Counselors, and Therapists, Las Vegas, NV, June.

Conley, T. D., Moors, A. C., Ziegler, A., & Karathanasis, C. (2012). Unfaithful individuals are less likely to practice safer sex than openly nonmonogamous individuals. *The Journal of Sexual Medicine, 9,* 1559–1565, doi: 10.1111/j.1743-6109.2012.02712.x.

Ferrer, J. N. (2007). Monogamy, polyamory, and beyond. *Tikkun, 22,* 37–62.

Fleckenstein, J. R., & Cox, D. W. (2015). The association of an open relationship orientation with health and happiness in a sample of older US adults. *Sexual and Relationship Therapy, 30,* 94–116.

Haupert, M., Gesselman, A., Moors, A., Fisher, H., & Garcia, J. (2016). Prevalence of experiences with consensual non-monogamous relationships: Findings from two nationally representative samples of single Americans. *Journal of Sex and Marital Therapy,* doi: 10.1080/0092623X.2016.1178675.

Henrich, R., & Trawinski, C. (2016). Social and relationship challenges facing polyamorous clients. *Sexual and Relationship Therapy.* Available at: http:/dx.doi.org/10.1080 /148681994.2016.117.4331

Kinsey, A. (1948). *Sexual behavior of the human male.* Bloomington: Indiana University Press.

Klesse, C. (2014). Polyamory: Intimate practice, identity or sexual orientation? *Sexualities, 17,* 81–89.

McLean, K. (2004). Negotiating nonmonogamy: Bisexuality and intimate relationships. *Journal of Bisexuality, 4,* 83–97, doi: 10.1300/J159v04n01_07.

Merriam-Webster. Consensual. Retrieved June 24, 2017 from www.merriam-webster. com/dictionary/consensual

Merriam-Webster. Polyamory. Retrieved June 24, 2017 from www.merriam-webster. com/dictionary/polyamory

Nichols, M. (2004). Lesbian sexuality/female sexuality: Rethinking "lesbian bed death." *Sexual and Relationship Therapy, 19,* 363–371.

O'Neill, N., & O'Neill, G. (1973). *Open marriage.* New York: Avon Books.

Orion, R. (2007). *Polyamory and the bisexual marriage.* Research report. San Francisco: Saybrook Graduate School and Research Center.

Orion, R. (2008a). *From traditional to open marriage.* Case study report. San Francisco: Saybrook Graduate School & Research Center.

Orion, R. (2008b). Polyamory as treatment for low desire. Paper presented at the Western Regional Conference of the Society for the Scientific Study of Sexuality, San Diego, CA, April.

Orion, R. (2011). Examining definitions and treatments of low desire and low-sex marriage (Doctoral dissertation). Available from ProQuest Dissertations and Theses Global database (Dissertation No. 3465923).

Sheff, E. A. (2014). *The polyamorists next door: Inside multiple relationships and families.* Lanham, MD: Rowman & Littlefield.

Sheff, E. A. (2017). Personal conversation with author, September 23.

Tweedy, A. E. (2011). Polyamory as a sexual orientation. *University of Cincinnati Law Review, 79,* 1461–1515.

Wasick-Correa, K. (2010). Agreements, rules and agentic fidelity in polyamorous relationships. *Psychology and Sexuality, 1,* 1. Available at: http:/dx.doi. org/10.1080/19419891003634471

Zell, M. (1990). A bouquet of lovers: Strategies for responsible open relationships. Available at: www.caw.org, *Church of All Worlds.* Article originally appeared in *Green Egg #89, Beltane 199.*

Part II
Issues and Interventions

4 Agreements, Boundaries, and Rules in Consensual Nonmonogamy

"Feelings of worth can flourish only in an atmosphere where individual differences are appreciated, mistakes are tolerated, communication is open, and rules are flexible—the kind of atmosphere that is found in a nurturing family." Wise words of Virginia Satir, humanistic psychologist. Traditional monogamous relationships have one seeming advantage when it comes to agreements, boundaries, and rules: Supposedly everyone already knows what to do. So what's there to discuss? Many modern couples recite ancient vows without questioning whether or not they each envision monogamy the same way. Spouses may later discover that their expectations and visions are quite different, even though they said the same words at marriage and believe that everyone knows what they mean.

Why do people get married, anyway? One reason relevant to this book is for assurance of security. Common belief is that love is the first and most important criterion, but it is the marriage ritual that puts love into a secure, committed context, making *this* love different from other loves. If it is a traditional marriage, unspoken assumed rules and boundaries are automatically considered part of the agreement. The marriage is the contract, the assurance, the pledge that allows partners to feel secure in their expectations of love, daily living, and future.

The Merriam-Webster dictionary defines "agreement" as "Unity of opinion, understanding, or intent; especially the mutual assent of contracting parties to the same terms if they reach agreement." I find that many married individuals have not discussed how their opinions, understandings, or intentions will play out in daily living. Have they truly reached *mutual assent* of the same terms? Often they believe so, without actually discussing aspects of expectations, assuming instead that "everyone knows" what a marriage commitment means. Boundaries and rules are presumed the same for everyone—and interpreted as manifesting in the same behaviors by everyone.

I have heard consensual nonmonogamous (CNM) partners say, "The whole point is not to control how people feel and what they do." This is an argument for loosely defined relationship restrictions. Those who espouse CNM values, or who simply love more than one person honestly, may feel that putting limits on freedom is an oxymoron. Some people are able to have successful, responsible relationships (with one or more persons) without much negotiation of agreements. Conversely, one study (Ramirez & Brown, 2010) shows that gay men in open relationships who have explicit rules with regard to having sex with other men are significantly more satisfied in their relationships than are control group men, who had no rules. Giving up the assumed rules of monogamy without espousing other guidelines creates a loosely defined free-for-all and may be a recipe for disaster.

Its not an either/or, however—either the closed structure of monogamy or a free-for-all. Greater sexual and emotional freedom allows passion, creativity, love, spirit, and hormones to flow, but may not lend to good thinking skills. Agreed upon boundaries and rules create a structure in which partners can enjoy individual personal freedoms while remaining safe and supporting the success of all relationships involved.

Consensual nonmonogamy clients may use the words *agreements, expectations, contracts, boundaries,* and *rules* interchangeably. I find it common for individuals to believe that their expectations comprise contracts, boundaries, or rules, and that these are the same as all other partners' expectations. Far from a consensus existing, individuals may not even have realized or examined their own expectations, let alone openly discussed them with others. Partners may be acting as if they are in a traditional commitment in which "everyone knows" what the rules are and is expected to follow them in the same manner as everyone else. Whether the relationship is two traditional partners or multiple partners in a nontraditional format, everyone seeks security—assurance of emotional safety and a definitive place in the relationship. To feel assurance, everyone needs confidence and ease.

Considering the definitions of these terms, there is variation in meaning and purpose between rules and boundaries, though both aim to limit behaviors for the greater good: for the outcome of security with freedom. True agreements cannot be made based on expectations but require *assent to terms* by all parties. A first priority in working with CNM clients is to clarify the expectations of each individual and their bases. Have partners discussed specific behaviors and activities that manifest the expectations of the group? Everyone needs some rules and boundaries to feel safe and to know what to do moment to moment.

Boundaries are guidelines with flexibility. They set general outlines for behaviors that work for the partnership, but which may be carried out with some fluidity to accommodate reality. *Rules* are a prescribed standard for regulation. Rules are necessary. If we didn't all stop at red lights, none of us would be safe. In relationships, I find that people often assume unarticulated rules as *accepted custom, procedure, or habit* (the definition of "rules" in the Merriam-Webster dictionary).

Consensual nonmonogamy is clearly not according to societal rule. Living in a CNM partnership requires clarity, communication, and creativity to form workable agreements, including whatever boundaries or rules may be needed. In my research and clinical experience, I have met clients who, during their years of CNM partnership, have settled into routines, with knowledge of what works and how to carry it out. In general, CNM practitioners may be no more gifted at awareness, communication, or creating clear agreements than anyone else. Some may have been swept into the lifestyle, or dove in and tried to figure out what they wanted and how to make it work through trial by fire—and perhaps have not yet gotten out of the fire.

Clients don't always know the source of problems that are causing complaint. Some announce what they *think* is wrong or may blame a certain person or reason. I find that when individuals or partners have an alternative going on, some throw everything into that bucket—*anything wrong must be because of CNM*. Others blame themselves for difficulties in relationships, citing a long-standing personal problem. My client Kitty thought her problems with CNM were entirely due to her history with anxiety.

When rules or boundaries are not working, these various causes may exist:

- There are practical reasons, such as time management, including schedules.
- Emotions may catalyze objections to practical arrangements (such as time allotments for each partner's shared time).
- A new partner may have entered the circle.
- Agreements may include rules or boundaries that are wrong for one partner although not for others.
- Agreements may include rules or boundaries that are difficult to follow.
- Individuals may have mental, emotional, or temperament problems, making CNM negotiations and agreements difficult for them.

Let's discuss how therapists can assess and intervene by doing the following:

- Clarify agreements, rules, or boundaries that are in place.
- Sort problems with agreements, rules, or boundaries vs. problems with individuals' personal issues.
- Work with each individual to provide support and resolve personal issues.
- Help redefine and fine-tune agreements.
- Facilitate clear discussion and teach communication skills.
- Recommend repeated sessions until consistent success is experienced.

Clarify Agreements, Rules, or Boundaries that Are in Place

Get a Picture of the Relationship

How many partners are there? What is the living situation? If there are children, whose are they? Are any negotiated and articulated agreements, rules, or boundaries in place? If so, what are they, and if not, why not?

Sue and her partner have a rule that they tell each other in advance "how far" they think they will go with a specific date that night. Kevin and Kitty have the rule that they share *friend-with-benefit* dates together as a couple, no individual outside dating. Many CNM folks have a rule that family scheduling comes first. If all partners do not have the same understanding—but think they do—this may be why some problems have occurred.

Define Terms

As part of working with clients to develop agreements, definition of terms needs to take place. For example, when partners try to create agreements, they may interchange *rules* and *boundaries*, and they may use important words like *loyalty*, *trust*, and *honesty*, among others, in different ways. Have all partners involved described behaviors they believe express such values and how they expect others to carry them out? A client, Sofie, provides an example:

> I feel betrayed by Sam. He had this conversation with my dad about why he [Sam] is staying alone at his trailer right now. I didn't know he'd said anything until my dad's girlfriend called to ask me why Sam and I are having problems. How can he just tell our private business? He knows it will come back to me. It's about loyalty—protecting me and us—it's no one's business!

Sam protested, saying he calls it honesty; he feels he has a right to talk about his problems with his father in-law, with whom he shares a friendly connection.

This couple, married for years, had never discussed what each considers to be *loyal* or *honest*. When problems arose in the marriage, differences in perspective and personal definitions became clear. I find it common for partners to relate based on nonvalidated assumptions and expectations.

CNM partners may have negotiated rules but find out there are problems when trying to carry these out, signaling a need to review agreements. Or as new situations arise, experiences may make it clear that new rules are needed.

Help Define the Basis for Rules and Boundaries

When partners do have agreements they all seem to understand, how did they achieve this? There may be good negotiation and communication skills among the group. Based upon what relationship or personal factors did partners create each agreement or rule: Who needed what, and how is the need answered by the resulting rule?

Jill and Jack in their *don't ask, don't tell* expanded monogamy arrangement had very few rules or boundaries. Their rules were *don't tell me what you're doing* and *don't schedule it when family is meant to come first*. They had little need to discuss other types of boundaries, since neither wanted to know about the other's outside partners, let alone have anything to do with choosing them.

Jill never sought extra partners, partly because one of her personal boundaries included not dating anyone near home and family. She had little opportunity to meet people elsewhere, even if she had wanted to.

Jack had several partners throughout his 29 years of open marriage, and he created some boundaries of his own with his other partners. He did not need one-night stands, strangers, drama, or people in rough emotional shape. He respected his wife's needs and the responsibility of family life. Other partners had to accept his wife and family as permanent in his life; partners must live and meet with him in places away from his family and home (which his job did allow him to do); partners had to observe sexual health and safety practices. And they had to be the kind of people he'd like anyway, if he were not married.

With all these rules, he feared he would never find partners. "The women are not just going to drop at my feet!" he once declared in a therapy session. But following his own rules over the years, he developed several relatively long-term secondary relationships with high-functioning people.

Sort Problems with Agreements, Rules, or Boundaries vs. Problems with Individuals' Personal Issues

A challenge in sorting out the practical from the personal is the overlap of issues in consensual nonmonogamy. Problems in one area, such as time and boundaries, may be intertwined with issues such as jealousy, personal difficulties of an individual, and psychosocial events in the lives of the group.

Rules can work if they can be reasonably followed, and if partners are clear on how to carry them out in various situations. As in the rest of life, things happen and rules cannot always apply, but they can be used as strong guidelines. Rather than rules, in some cases, boundaries—the concept of flexible guidelines—are more realistic.

A good example is the woman who told her spouse, "You can have sexual fun at parties as long as it doesn't involve your penis." She is trying to create a rule that won't trigger her jealousy. She thinks that if he doesn't involve his penis, their relationship is still secure or special even though they allow some sexual play with others.

Her husband had difficulty following this rule. In practice, what does this rule mean? If he kisses someone or fondles breasts, that is OK according to the rule. When he gets an erection from these activities, his penis is involved. Must he then stop any arousing activity until he loses his erection? Is it OK for him to go to the bathroom and masturbate to relieve himself? If his party-fun partner sees the erection, the rule would dictate that neither she nor he engage in any touch or sexual activity with the penis. What if he gives oral sex to the woman at the party? That does not involve his penis, but it is certainly an intimate sex act that may lead to orgasm for her, and possibly for him even if he doesn't deliberately use his penis. The situation is frustrating for him and asks him to resist unreasonable temptation as well as to act unnaturally. The rule may be disrespectful of the woman at the party. She may be embarrassed or insulted that she can otherwise touch and kiss and cuddle with this man, but don't touch the penis! Is he supposed to rush home to have sex with his wife the minute he gets so excited that he wants to "involve his penis?"

Not only is this rule unclear and difficult to follow sensibly, but it is specious in terms of providing security to his wife with regard to their relationship. Security must come from within each person and each partnership, not from attempts to control specific minute behaviors of partners in sexual situations with others. This rule is based more on the wife's insecurities than on trust and respect or any realistic threat to health or safety. This woman and her husband need to revamp their rules and boundaries, examining their definitions of *trust* and *respect*. They need to discover why they do want a sexually open relationship, and if so, both must be clear about their reasons.

A similar rule often heard is that it's OK to have sex with other people, but not to love them. Limiting outside sex to casual dates and unemotional liaisons can work, but individuals cannot control whom they may end up loving. Love does not listen to rules. CNM clients frequently present problems when one partner's *friend-with-benefits* or casual sex date becomes an important person to that partner, and the two fall in love. "I never wanted polyamory!" the first partner complains. "We agreed that outside sex was just for fun. It shouldn't compete with *our* relationship!"

In general, rules attempting to control the uncontrollable will not be successful. Such rules may reflect personal problems of individual partners or may indicate that a partner is not comfortable with or suited for consensual nonmonogamy.

Expanded monogamy relationships based on unemotional outside sex can work for years without either partner falling in love unexpectedly. When falling in love does happen, in theory, a second love relationship does not compete with the first.

Matt, Angela, and Juan are a good example. Matt and Angela are married. Matt is bisexual. Angela knows this, and until Matt met Juan there was no issue. Angela and Matt have few boundaries around feelings; they know this is something one cannot control. Angela wants to know any partners of Matt's, however, and doesn't want him to engage in anonymous and random sexual activities with other males, due to safety and health reasons. Her rules, he agrees.

Then Matt fell in love with Juan, another bisexual man married to a woman. Juan is a friend and gets to know Angela; they all share many activities. Unexpectedly Angela and Juan fall in love as well. Now boundaries about feelings become an issue. Each partner has special feelings for the other, and each relationship needs some time without the third person involved. Juan could not just move in with Matt and Angela due to his own family circumstances, so they start scheduling and dealing with who might have stronger feelings for whom and how often each pair needs time. Angela feels strongly that she and Matt still need married time as the couple they have always been.

This triad went through a lot of permutations and got help sorting up and being creative, before figuring out some of the logistics of their complicated and intense relationships. They were swept into their situation, which they state was "the best time of our lives, we all love each other, and despite the challenges we wouldn't give up this time for anything."

Polyamorous folks know that more than one meaningful relationship can function well simultaneously for those who can manage jealousy and truly accept that each relationship is unique and valuable. Time-sharing becomes an issue; dealing with feelings as part of resolving issues is necessary. But love is not limited, and loving another person does not take love from the first. Love with a new or second person can enhance and enliven a long-term or primary relationship. Conversely, it is possible that love with the first was already waning; if so, that must be perceived as a separate aspect.

Most CNM practitioners state that one reason they want open relationships is to allow for more pleasure, fun, excitement, and—if polyamorous—love, friendship, and spiritual connection. These are all emotions eliciting powerful chemicals in the human brain and body. Emotions and energies are not all under human control, but behaviors ought to be. Individuals don't have to act on every emotion and should not, but rules and boundaries need to be realistic. Some rules can be followed regardless of emotions involved, such as those providing health and safety.

Start with What's Easy

Assessing logistical arrangements may yield straightforward practical problems with practical solutions. Mandy explained that one reason she had problems enjoying intimate time with Candy was that the kids' bedrooms are just down the hall. "There's no lock on our door. The kids are 7 and 9 now, they don't often need to run into our room in the night, but we've always left our door ajar just in case. We've never considered a lock!"

Mandy sounded shocked at the very idea of assuring some privacy, but she could accept that her children are old enough to knock and wait a moment if they need their parents during date night. These partners' complaints about their sex life were greatly reduced after installation of a simple lock.

Personal Problems

When practical solutions don't correct problems, the understanding and experiences of individual partners must be considered. People bring all of themselves into relationships. Whether one partner or many, every individual has a unique blend of self, including relationship skills and problems. Overriding issues with one partner can impact how agreements are carried out on a daily basis. Assessment and approaches for individuals are no different in CNM than in monogamy. Common problems may have compound effects and may need to be addressed by all partners, however.

One studied factor, low self-esteem, is a relatively common problem and can wreak havoc in trying to make CNM work. Righetti and Visserman (2017) report research findings that persons with low self-esteem "often make relationship sacrifices that they believe are unappreciated. The regret can cause more negative mood, greater stress, and lower life satisfaction over time." CNM relationships require more compromise and sacrifices by partners than monogamous relationships. Low self-esteem makes jealousy and other CNM challenges especially difficult to manage. A person with low self-esteem is likely to have problems following even simple agreements made for practicality, such as a schedule of partners' time together.

According to researcher Francesca Righetti (2017):

> Low self-esteem partners desire strong interpersonal connections like everybody else but they are very sensitive to rejection and interpersonal threats. They underestimate how positively they are viewed by their partner and how much [s/he] loves and cares for them . . . [they perceive] that others are not there for them [when support is needed].

Work with Each Individual to Provide Support and Resolve Personal Issues

With so many personal issues possibly inherent in any client, and therefore multiplied in CNM relationships, how can it be ascertained if issues are about boundaries and rules alone, or about personal issues? Work with each partner as with any individual client. Issues present for individuals in consensual nonmonogamy are the same as for any other person who comes for therapy. The usual list of contributors to problems must be examined, including background and physical and mental health issues. These may underlie rules or boundary choices—or inability to follow them.

It is understandable for anyone to feel insecure, at least sometimes, in a multiple relationship. Someone with low self-esteem likely struggles with insecurity routinely. Whether with one or more partners, self-esteem affects the ability to relate successfully.

Researcher Righetti's advice regarding low self-esteem persons in relationships supports what I recommend, and what I see successfully practiced by some CNM partners: Show clear and strong appreciation and gratitude for efforts made by partners. This is a good rule for all partners, regardless of their self-esteem level.

The low self-esteem partner, however, may have difficulty in accepting appreciation. I call this *seeing through crap-colored glasses*. No matter how much love and appreciation is shown, a person cannot see it. They need help taking off those glasses and believing what their partners are actually saying. Clients with low self-esteem must be assisted to question their own assumption that partners do not notice what they do for the relationship. They need help in learning to accept that their partners are telling the truth and that partners truly value them. Achieving this may require individual therapy for that person. Partners may also need help showing appreciation and support to this person who is unused to seeing it.

Many a client has told me how bad they feel about the problems in their relationship, which they assume are caused by their own issues. Yet exploration reveals that their self-reported personal issue is not the base of the problem. Kitty blamed all her problems with expanded monogamy marriage on her anxiety. She wanted to please her husband, Kevin, who was clear before marriage that he required consensual nonmonogamy. Kitty had overcome her GAD (Generalized Anxiety Disorder) and is doing well, living all other aspects of her life without anxiety. Kitty often enjoyed their couples shared sex parties and would initiate planning and organizing them. "But then," she lamented:

> after I'm there, I get drunk, upset, and try to ruin the date for everyone. It's my fault. I should be able to handle this! I don't know why I can't apply my tools for overcoming anxiety to this situation.

"And I'm going nuts because she says *yes*, and does *no*," complains Kevin.

Kitty needed to hear that one reason she is unable to apply her tools is because she imbibes alcohol. As soon as she is drinking, her ability to think and make alternate behavior choices is impaired. I asked Kitty whether she felt anxiety before or after she started drinking. "Oh . . . I hadn't thought about that. It can go either way!"

Kitty sometimes felt anticipatory anxiety. As party plans drew near, she suppressed feelings of fear that she would again feel bad once at the party. Rather than preparing to use her anxiety calming skills, she would start drinking the minute she arrived at the party. Other times she realized that she wouldn't get drunk until she started to feel bad. In either case, she was not dealing with feelings and triggers that set off her anxiety and was self-medicating with alcohol instead.

More triggers to anxiety may exist in open and multiple relationships than in other areas of a person's life. To help Kitty pinpoint triggers so she can deal with them rather than pick up a drink, I elicit more information about what happens at these parties: what Kitty does with whom; when exactly does she get upset, and what is happening at that moment in the room. Where is Kevin when Kitty first notices her upset?

Problems experienced with her *couples-friends-with-benefits* sex dates might be solved by modifying some rules and boundaries that Kitty and Kevin had loosely created but never reviewed. To help pinpoint problems with rules or boundaries, ask for any details relevant to the client and the situation.

Help Redefine and Fine-Tune Agreements

Fine-tune agreements, rules, and boundaries to provide support and protect true needs of individuals and of each relationship. Make sure children's needs are not only considered, but are the first priority.

"How did that go?" I asked Mandy in a follow-up session. She's been having problems seeing Candy when Candy gets home from dates with men. Mandy understands the need for, and agrees to, their open sexual agreement, but is not reacting well when this is carried out.

Mandy had come up with the idea that she stay in the guesthouse on the nights of Candy's dates. This allowed Candy some space after her dates to get centered, refocused on home and marriage, and shower off her night before seeing Mandy. Mandy was able to stay connected to her own mental and physical space, rather than feeling that Candy's dates were "in my face—and nose."

"It helps," Mandy replied to my inquiry.

> There's still some tension the next day but it's much less than it was. I feel that over time I'll get used to it, and I enjoy the guesthouse, actually! It's like a night out for me and the kids in a quiet, luxurious place. We remodeled it for family and friends, but why not enjoy it ourselves?

Therapists must assess how arrangements and adjustments are working. If a partner is reactionary and emotional to another when an agreed-upon event has taken place, that partner needs to learn calm "I" language and active listening, rather than blowing up or arguing.

In essence, partners need to learn in their own way to say, *I've been having trouble following this rule . . . I understand it, but in real life I can't carry it out. I respect your need for this boundary. How else might we do this? What else can we try?* When the client doesn't know how to communicate like this, clinicians model and teach.

Kitty, in a session of her own, offered details about getting upset at her and Kevin's sex parties. The issue emerged that Kevin ignored Kitty as soon as they arrived at parties and joined their friends. "It's like I'm not even there," she explained. Her description revealed that Kevin essentially shut her out emotionally and physically while with other partners, even when they were just socializing together before anyone has sex. At the same time she witnessed his intense attention on someone else.

A rule might be developed about how much or in what ways Kevin stays with Kitty, or pays attention to her, at their parties. Kevin needs to be more compassionate and attentive to his wife—at least acknowledge and include her in his conversations when they are on "play dates." Kevin complained, "But that's the whole point! It's freedom! Not to have to worry about anybody and just go with whatever you feel for another partner." Kevin can't control his emotions and wants to enjoy the reason he and Kitty partake of such parties. But he needs to learn to support and be respectful toward his wife in order for their marriage to benefit, rather than be damaged, from the lifestyle.

Kitty and Kevin worked hard together to find safe, acceptable partners and to schedule dates around many life responsibilities. But Kevin wants no boundaries at parties and Kitty needs some. So here we have the issue of *complete freedom* vs. *safe boundaries and reasonable relationship rules.*

Kevin appears to want complete and total freedom to do whatever he wants, no matter whom it hurts. I don't think anyone will knowingly agree to that. I don't think Kevin really wants it. It sounds as if what he wants is to do anything he feels in the moment and have it bother no one. That's a great feeling when it works, but that kind of complete freedom, including the use of drugs, alcohol, and multiple sexual liaisons, doesn't match well with being a parent and being in a marriage—even an open one.

One rule needs to be that Kitty and Kevin control their drinking at parties, as they both state that they are drunk before most problems arise. Then arguments

ensue because neither one is calm or sober enough to talk reasonably. They take ·
precautions never to drive home drunk, but fail to protect themselves and their
relationship from the damaging and dangerous effects of alcohol. Do you want
to stay alive when drinking? Don't get behind a wheel. Want your relationship
to survive? Limit alcohol consumption *significantly*, especially in situations where
triggers to problems may occur. This is an example of a practical measure that
immediately solves or reduces many problems. CNM is a privilege, not permission to act irresponsibly, dangerously, or *care-less-ly* to others.

Another adjustment to this couple's rules may be for Kitty to *see* less of Kevin's
amorous feelings directed elsewhere. He and his party friend can wait until they
have time alone behind a closed door. Kitty and Kevin could also decide to allow
each other to go alone on some individual dates with known partners. Other
options and responses may arise through facilitated discussion.

Facilitate Clear Discussion and Teach Communication Skills

"We have problems with communication." This sentence is likely heard routinely
in any therapist's office. Often it means, "We argue a lot"—and resolve little.
Multiply by several partners and uncharted circumstances, and you have consensual nonmonogamy.

Success in CNM requires a lot of communication, all the time. Awareness of
feelings, speaking from the self in a relatively calm manner, listening, compassion,
appreciation, confidence, and other skills are required. Most of us did not have
classes in communication as we were growing up, and many people have poor
models to learn from. As a therapist, my exposure is limited and may be skewed,
but it's the smaller percentage of clients in 17 years of my practice who have
sophisticated communication and relationship skills when they walk in my door.
Some who do, learned such skills through previous therapy or other educational
experiences.

While communication skills are necessary to every aspect of relationships and
all the issues discussed in this book, negotiating agreements is an area most
demanding in CNM. Even when discussing practicalities such as a schedule,
emotional issues may arise. Busy parents in any family must communicate regularly about many activities and obligations; in CNM, add managing quality time
for all adult partners and negotiating rules and boundaries of how to spend that
time. Since no one's life plays out like clockwork, everyone fares better with the
ability to regularly and continuously speak about daily living plans and keeping
partnerships clear of unresolved issues.

The specific communication skills needed in CNM are no different from those
best practiced by any individual in any partnership, but the number of things
to discuss and plan—many emotionally charged—are multiplied. In my field
research (2007, 2008, 2011), I asked participants if they had advice for others
who are trying to make consensual nonmonogamy work. At the top of the list
for all participants is communicate, communicate, communicate! Stay aware of
feelings and how arrangements are working. Check in with partners. Express

gratitude and appreciation verbally as well as in other ways. Staying calm and sharing organized thoughts is best for any relationship, but crucial in CNM where so many triggers to feelings may occur.

Once practical arrangements are set up, keeping in touch and checking in may become the most of what is needed. Some partners find ways to minimize the need for communicating all the time, such as Jill's "family calendar" she created to minimize discussion of when Jack could schedule liaisons that Jill didn't want to know about. Jill and Jack wanted a *don't ask, don't tell* arrangement precisely because they did not want to intertwine their outside relationships with their family life and discussions. Jill had no interest in knowing or hearing about Jack's other relationships, nor did she want to discuss her own (or lack thereof). This couple got clear on the few rules each felt strong about (health and safety, preserving family time, and not discussing other partners), and then rarely spoke of their open agreement in 29 years of successful marriage. Even with this set-up, Jack stated in a research interview that he wished he'd checked in more often and made sure how everything was working for Jill. The few times any issue came up regarding scheduling or relationships, it was Jill who initiated the conversation. She said she was not upset about that fact, because Jack listened and made changes immediately to their arrangements when she did bring any problem to light.

Many CNM partners have check-in "family meetings" once a week. This gives all partners an arena and a planned time to voice feelings and bring up problems with arrangements, rules, and boundaries.

Exemplifying a couple who succeeds through ongoing communication are Sanjay and Anita. They are swingers and regularly have dinner with various prospective couples. While their relationships with these people are limited to sex and a pleasant evening, Anita and Sanjay have a number of rules and boundaries in place. They consider themselves a couple and come across that way. They don't want to all have sex in the same room; each couple is given privacy. Anita is choosier (possibly has better instincts about people) and insists that she has final approval of any couple they exchange with—even if Sanjay likes them and she doesn't. He is allowed to search for prospective couples online and through other venues, and she will go with his pick to be invited for a meet and greet coffee. Sanjay did ask Anita to reconsider a certain couple that he liked that she had kyboshed. They talked about it, and she agreed to meet with them again, which changed her opinion of them.

Although each has received offers, they have a rule not to date individually partners of other couples. They have privacy with others during their evenings all together, but Anita shares that the husband in one of their dates invited her out solo several times before she convinced him that she was sticking to the rules she and Sanjay had set. Sanjay has asked Anita a couple of times if he could accept an invitation similar to those Anita received, and she had to stand firm and say no, she's not comfortable with changing their rule. So far, he's not felt strongly enough about anyone else, nor wanted to damage his relationship with Anita, to find that keeping their rule is a problem.

As long as both Sanjay and Anita follow their rules and boundaries, they seem to end up with discreet partners with whom both feel safe. They have to communicate a lot about prospective dates, and they check in with each other as to how it went without wanting to know everything.

"I respect her absolutely," Sanjay vehemently declared.

> She's usually right about people. I've been hurt and in danger once from a couple I thought was fine. They were a little nuts! I'm grateful that Anita is into this, too. It's a really strong thing between us that we both understand this [lifestyle]. But I can talk to her, we have to talk!

Even in such well-functioning CNM relationships, feelings can flare unexpectedly. Teach "I" language, compassionate listening, active listening, anger management, dealing with jealousy—whatever is needed for any individual or set of partners.

Recommend Repeated Sessions Until Consistent Success with Arrangements Is Experienced

It takes time for new skills and changes to take firm hold. This also applies to the creation of, changes in, or additions to rules and boundaries. I find many clients stop coming in as soon as things are going better or some issues are resolving. Clinicians know that this is often too soon for people to stop therapy and relapses may occur. With more partners, sex, and emotions involved in CNM, it is important to stress the value of continued therapy check-ins, possibly with decreasing frequency. It may be valuable to see individual partners alone for some sessions as well.

Over time, those who cannot feel comfortable and manage this lifestyle, no matter what is tried, need help considering whether CNM is really correct for them. It may not be, even if those individuals agree with the values and want CNM to work.

References

Merriam-Webster. Agreement. Retrieved June 25, 2017, from www.merriam-webster.com/dictionary/agreement

Merriam-Webster. Rule. Retrieved June 25, 2017, from www.merriam-webster.com/dictionary/rule

Orion, R. (2007). *Polyamory and the bisexual marriage*. Research report, San Francisco: Saybrook Graduate School and Research Center.

Orion, R. (2008). *From traditional to open marriage*. Case study report. San Francisco: Saybrook Graduate School & Research Center.

Orion, R. (2011). Examining definitions and treatments of low desire and low-sex marriage (Doctoral dissertation). Available from ProQuest Dissertations and Theses Global database (Dissertation No. 3465923).

Ramirez, O. M., & Brown, J. (2010). Attachment style, rules regarding sex, and couple satisfaction: A study of gay male couples. *Australian and New Zealand Journal of Family Therapy*, *31* (2), 202–213, doi: 10.1375/anft.31.2.202.

Righetti, F., & Visserman, M. (2017). I gave too much: Low self-esteem and the regret of sacrifices. *Social Psychological and Personality Science*, online before print May 16, 2017. Available at: www.spsp.org/news-center/press-releases/relationship-sacrifice

Satir, V. Retrieved May 27, 2017, from https://www.brainyquote.com/quotes/quotes/v/virginiasa175186.html?src=t_rules

Case Excerpt: Jill and Jack

This excerpt reports on 26 years of the consensually nonmonogamous marriage of Jill and Jack. Each worked with me as a voluntary research participant. Jill had several client sessions over a period of years. Their marriage was originally a traditional monogamous one. After 3 years they created a *don't ask, don't tell* agreement that continues to be successful. This case has been presented at scientific sexuality conferences and has relevant discussion following.

At first interview, Jill and Jack have been married for 3 years. They're both in their mid-thirties and have a 2-year-old son. Jack is employed as an engineer with a second successful career as a consultant. Jill is a full-time mother and has a small home business. Jill estimates that she does 80% of the childcare and housework, while Jack provides 80% of the income. Both express satisfaction with this situation.

This couple married for the same reasons reported by many: to be intimate partners, create a home, and have children. They intended to live monogamously. They were in love and good friends. They are an excellent match "on paper": similar backgrounds and daily living habits, values, and goals. Both state that in their past, they had had more exciting sexual partners than one another, but that those sexual partners would not have made good spouses. Each thought that their mediocre sexual relationship would be outweighed by other similarities and advantages of marriage.

They soon discovered that their lack of sexual chemistry was more of a problem than anticipated. Jill, never as interested in sexual activity as Jack, became even less so after their child was born. As a few years passed, attempts to develop a satisfactory sexual connection, including with professional help, failed. Jack experienced growing physical and emotional stress; Jill experienced guilt and anxiety about their marriage. Both state they were at the point of divorce, and would have divorced, if they had not tried an open marriage.

Jack said he would prefer to have sex with his own wife. But faced with three choices—Jill forcing herself to have unwanted sex, Jack going without sex completely, or a divorce—Jill and Jack both preferred a less conventional option: that Jack seek outside partners for sexual activity. Since Jack travels for his consulting job, he has opportunity to meet with women while already absent from home.

They both report experiences typical among couples I've researched in this situation: relief from pressures and guilt, acceptance of their true selves, caring and respect for their partner's needs, a renewed sense of freedom and connection between them, and personal growth and change.

They also report typical problems of the *don't ask, don't tell* arrangement. Jill experienced over time a sense of inadequacy and feeling undesirable. She compared herself unfavorably to unknown women. Jill felt Jack was away from family even more due to seeing other women. When Jill expressed her dissatisfaction about timesharing, however, Jack responded positively and adhered to a schedule they made for family time and activities.

Jack reports that although he was consistently adamant in honesty about remaining married, some of his lovers were emotionally closer to him than was his wife. He experienced some difficulty in finding partners who would accept his situation, but over a period of 6 years, he had several relatively long-term lovers.

Jealousy is a common issue in nearly all CNM situations. Jill thinks she limited her jealousy by knowing nothing about Jack's other relationships and, she stated, she would use forgiveness and understanding to ameliorate her feelings.

Jack states he doesn't know if he'd be jealous of his wife's outside partners, because she consistently chose not to pursue any, although she had equal right to do so. He declared, "If she could find pleasure with someone else, I wish that she would! I feel she misses something in life, and I am grateful that she works with me like this, so I don't have to miss that aspect."

Jack explained that he did experience extreme jealousy with one of his lovers, who did not see Jack exclusively and was quite open about her other partners. Jack experienced two extremes on the CNM openness continuum—a partner at home with whom he shared practically no intimate details, and a partner outside the home who shared almost everything about her lovers.

When their son was in school, 6 years into their CNM arrangement, they separated for a year, thinking they might divorce. Both reiterate that CNM was not the reason, but instead, the issues and problems that they struggled with from the beginning of their marriage, coupled with social pressure.

Jill's already low sexual self-esteem did not improve, and she reports a complaint common to many long-term partners: Over time they had less genuine sharing and growth when they were together. Jack expressed a preference for a single partner with whom he shares sexual compatibility, if that were possible. He felt increasingly like an adulterer despite the open agreement, partly because of what friends said to him when they discovered that Jack had a CNM arrangement. Jack also felt that he was in the way of Jill finding someone more suitable to her, since he continued to play the role of live-in husband, and Jill, while appearing to be traditionally married, felt uncomfortable looking for partners in the networks of people in her life.

Over the years, it was impossible to completely hide Jack's other partnerships and liaisons. A work friend saw Jack with a lover when on an out-of-town business trip. Both Jill and Jack experienced social stigma, which they state as one direct cause of their separation. Jill's few friends who knew about the CNM arrangement told her Jack was using her for housework while getting his sex elsewhere (a rather nonfeminist evaluation, in my opinion). This view devalues Jill's genuine enjoyment of motherhood, ignores both her lack of interest in sex and Jack's responsible commitment to his home and family. Jack's few friends who knew claimed that while they understood his situation, they "didn't like to see someone have sex outside their marriage."

A build-up of these personal and social pressures brought them to the decision to separate. Jack moved across the street and maintained his usual schedule of family time and home care with his son.

A year after separating, Jack moved back into the house with Jill. They had discovered that they didn't want to divorce, and that they wanted the rest of their lives together to be different than before the separation.

Jill took steps to meet others by posting on polyamory dating sites. Their intention was to create a more equal open arrangement. Jill never actually sought nor found another partner, but she became comfortable with the fact that she just isn't interested, and that Jack is. She doesn't know when Jack sees others, but she feels secure and no longer wonders very often about it.

As advice to others who consider an open relationship, Jill stated that while she did not choose to have other partners, it might be easier for others if they do. She found patience and forgiveness to be valuable attributes.

Jack says he would tell others to keep checking in over time, that he never looked back to reexamine or modify their arrangements. He feels he ought to have taken the initiative to do so, even though he responded positively when his wife brought up any issue. He emphasized that he has the highest regard for his wife and that mutual respect is essential.

They are happy with their lives, with the fact that they had a stable family environment for their son (now in college). They state that they "would have divorced years back" had they not accepted their differences and negotiated a compromise, however nontraditional or challenging.

Each expresses pride that they managed this nontraditional arrangement. The years living together with their son before the one-year separation had a positive impact on his life, during which time Jill and Jack experienced personal growth. Each state they love and respect the other, that when they separated it was amicable because of their open arrangement, and that they remained good friends and parents throughout. Opening their marriage, they state, kept them together to the date of this writing, and they have plans for buying a summer retirement home. Their son has never known about the CNM arrangement.

Discussion: Why Did CNM Work for This Couple?

- Both Jill and Jack are liberally educated and grew up during a time of social change that allowed them to consider unusual arrangements.
- They are committed to marriage as a partnership in family and survival. While sex was thought to be an automatic part of their marriage, they do not consider it the hinge of their commitment.

- They respect and understand each other as individuals—that one of them could find sex very important to well-being, the other not. Each was willing to accept the needs of the other and negotiate a compromise even about such a personal area as sex.
- They got professional help to improve their marriage in every way possible, including from a sex therapist. This helped them to determine that in their case, even when other relationship issues were resolved, sex was not going to automatically (or by creation) be there for them. In addition, they first tried everything recommended to solve the problem within their marriage. This helped them consider being different.
- They made changes in their CNM arrangement as needed.
- Each kept faithfully to their arrangements and commitments.
- Their lives were conducive to the *don't ask, don't tell* format. Jill wasn't interested in pursuing other relationships, although she may have had difficulty finding partners discreetly, had she wanted to, since she did not travel much. Jack did travel, and was able to maintain honest relationships with others over the years, without being near home or his family's circle of friends, which was part of their agreement.
- They paid attention to their own relationship as a priority.
- Neither one had mental or physical health issues that negatively impacted their relationship, or their own ability to deal with jealousy, communication, compromise, or personal growth.
- Their arrangement caused no negative impact on their family or child, but did significantly support the couple's ability to stay together in a happy, healthy, and financially stable situation, providing the same for their child. They knew how to keep adult issues to themselves, rather than having drama spilling over into the home and family.

5 Helping Jealous Clients

A common thought among those who are consensual nonmonogamists is "If you pass along love, you find that rather than being depleted, love multiplies" (Anonymous, posted on "hippie peace freaks" Facebook page, June 25, 2016). A common misconception about consensual nonmonogamy (CNM) is that people who accept such relationships don't feel jealous. Some people may not be suited for honest multipartnering, but my research (Orion, 2007, 2008, 2011) and clinical experience reveal that for those who have experience and skill in dealing honestly with more than one significant relationship, many report feeling jealousy at times, or even frequently. Among CNM clients, managing jealousy is one of the most commonly presented issues.

Jealous feelings and behavior are possibly even more common in monogamous relationships. I've heard many people in sexually monogamous relationships say they could never share their partner, they'd be too jealous. Jealousy less frequently or vehemently displayed may be considered a sign of love. A familiar client complaint is, "She (or he) wasn't even jealous when I flirted. She (or he) doesn't care about me any more."

Whether poly or monoamorous, jealousy is destructive. Individuals obsess mentally and cause damage to themselves, others, and relationships. Jealousy can break up otherwise workable partnerships.

The Merriam-Webster dictionary definition of jealousy includes as components of being jealous *hostile, intolerant, suspicious,* and *vigilant.* Similar to *envious,* jealousy has an aspect for individuals of feeling *less than*—less than whatever that other person must have more of, or must do better than, they. There is a fear of being value-less and the loss of something very important; hence, the need to guard it vigilantly. Jealousy is about fear of loss, feeling a threat to security within a relationship, and questioning self-worth.

These are miserable feelings for anyone to have! And hardly healthy or positive components of any relationship, regardless of the number of partners involved. CNM partners may be as equally clueless about managing jealousy as anyone else. Multiply the number of partners with feelings and varying levels of communication and other skills, and you have CNM.

Jealousy feels painful and causes pain. Individuals must be willing to learn to overcome jealousy if relationships are to be successful. In consensual nonmonogamy, love, honesty, and freedom are valued over jealousy. Difficult feelings are to be supported and examined; personal growth is required; partners help each other do both. When the individual can share directly underlying feelings (as opposed to reacting to triggers), partners can then directly reassure and soothe the person. How to reassure and soothe may vary. All partners have to figure out what helps any of them repair and keep going. The aim is for each partner to manage jealousy well enough so that it does not impair relationships or daily living.

Let's examine the following assessments and interventions useful for clinicians when one or more partners need help with jealousy:

- Assess the relationship format, perceived causes of jealousy, and precipitating incidents.
- Teach skills for managing ongoing jealousy.
- Help partners find ways of keeping jealousy to a minimum.
- Use techniques for healing jealousy.
- Teach *compersion* as a personal development.
- Use other clinical interventions generally found helpful in dealing with jealousy.

Assess the Relationship Format, Perceived Causes of Jealousy, and Precipitating Incidents

What is the format of the CNM relationships? Is there a married or central couple? Do they live traditionally and have "outside" partners, or are they part of a live-in *throuple, fourple,* or other group format? Clients may or may not use these labels (see Chapter 3), but if they do, it's important to accept the terms and use them in discussion. Do they live alone and have a network of lovers and friends? This gives an idea of how many personalities are involved on a daily basis, possible questions to ask, and what kinds of interventions may help.

Once known how many partners are involved, ascertain how much of the jealousy problem belongs to each as an individual. Does anyone say that jealousy has always been a problem? I find that many clients report honestly their own or a partner's level of jealousy.

It is useful to deconstruct the feelings and thoughts that comprise the state of being jealous. I believe the degree to which individuals feel jealous depends upon one or more of the following:

- instinct (part of the fight or flight response to protect territory or resources);
- cultural socialization and family of origin;
- temperament;
- background, including relationship and sexual experience;
- beliefs and values;
- mental and physical health;
- level of self-esteem.

In addition to causes for an individual's jealousy, it is important to determine if precipitating events, incidents, or behaviors involving jealousy (such as arguments, new person involved, repeated behaviors around certain activities) are cited as cause for seeking help right now. Is jealousy an ongoing struggle, or is it relatively manageable or unusual, with a recent significant event that brought clients in for help?

Teach Skills for Managing Ongoing Jealousy

In any relationship, individuals are responsible for their behavior. Someone with an anger problem has to learn anger management. A couple who argues a lot has to learn what I call "argument interruptus" and get help dealing with the underlying issues and with developing better communication. Every partner needs to become aware of personal feelings, learning how and when to share them effectively. Feelings may indicate that something about a situation needs tweaking or changing. The individual may need understanding and help to feel better.

If jealousy is a frequent or ongoing problem, get a picture of what's going on with regard to feelings, communication about, and management of jealousy. *So when that happened, what did you do about it?* How do individuals and partners express and respond to jealousy? Those partners who struggle may need to get more help and do more work to grow out of feeling frequently jealous, as well as to learn thought-stopping, positive self-talk, calming, and communication skills. These and other approaches (often used to manage anxiety) are useful.

Many people report that when jealous, they or their partner become insulting or even abusive. Often I hear that one or both partners have been drinking when feelings and outbursts get out of control. Either they had too much at a sexual party or liaison with secondary partners, or drank later and let their problematic feelings explode in a partner's face. I say to clients, *Keep "mean" behaviors under control! Don't drink more than a glass or two (know your own limit). Alcohol invariably leads to problems. Be responsible!*

Those who engage in consensual nonmonogamy must learn to control behaviors reasonably during shared or outside sexual situations, just as anyone must when angry, anxious, or jealous, even if they have to excuse themselves and leave the situation. If they act fine at the party or when a liaison is occurring, but blow up at their partner(s) later, that is not appropriate either. After all, partners had agreed on permission to participate.

It is not unusual for feelings to change or for partners to experience something unexpected, even though they were on board for sex with additional partners. These clients need to get clear about their own feelings and share those when sober and calm, asking for understanding and reassurance. Individuals must learn about themselves and their behavior; partners need to work together as an intimate team and get help if needed with communications skills and compassionate response. Meanwhile they start with limiting drugs and alcohol and keeping tempers and arguments under control.

Consensual nonmonogamy relationships that work involve people who are able to accept rather than avoid jealousy, self-soothe, and learn positive ways to share feelings and reconnect with each partner. This all helps jealousy come up less frequently. It is also helpful for persons who feel jealous to understand what may trigger their feelings and how to minimize those triggers. Journaling in the moment when jealous about physical and emotional feelings and specific thoughts can be illuminating and provide tools.

The story of James, Jenna, and Martin illustrates how to handle jealousy positively. They didn't always know how; they learned over time. Martin was not their first partner. Some previous partners could not handle well the complications of open multiple relationships.

James, part of a polyfidelitous throuple, has been married to and living with Jenna for 19 years. Martin has been a full-time third partner, including intimately with Jenna, for 7 years. The three see each other daily and they are all friends. James and Martin have well-developed arrangements for sharing time with Jenna. All three say their arrangements work, including separate times for each male to share activities, intimacy, and sex with Jenna. The following is an excerpt from an in-depth research interview with James:

> Even though I'm totally used to this [CNM relationships], and honestly I don't feel jealous or upset very often. I don't even think about it, this is just our lives. I love Martin, he's family. But a while back, I don't remember exactly when it was . . . it was Jenna and Martie's night together. We'd all been watching something and I got tired and left to get ready for bed. On my way back from the bathroom I saw them in the living room and it just hit me—the way they looked at each other, the energy between them. I mean it's been years! And I was suddenly devastated. I ran to the bedroom and cried. I was shocked. They must have heard me, they came in and were really comforting. They sat on the bed with me and we talked it out. I realized I suddenly wondered what I meant to her then. Why was I special? They seemed to have so much between them. They both took time out of their night to reassure me, they understood my feelings. And we all talked about why we care about each other, and why each of us, each relationship, is important and special. It's really unusual for me to even notice, I'm glad for them, I go off and do my own thing on their nights and forget all about it! That night turned out to be . . . it made us all closer, and I haven't felt jealous like that since.

Help Partners Find Ways of Keeping Jealousy to a Minimum

Some try to minimize jealousy by restricting what their partner(s) can do with or feel about others. Monogamous relationships come inherent with rules and boundaries, but CNM partners make up their own, sometimes in response to jealousy or in attempts to prevent it. *You can have sex with that person but you can't love her (or him)*, for example. Limitations, however, may make people feel falsely secure and often are impossible to carry out (see Chapter 4). In my experience, too many or certain types of rules and boundaries do not help minimize jealousy.

A sense of feeling left out makes some partners think that they will be less jealous if they hear every detail about their partner's other relationship and liaisons. Clients recovering from affairs in sexually monogamous relationships often think that the more they know about the "other woman" or man, the more details they learn about what the cheating spouse did with the secret partner, the better they, the betrayed spouse, will feel. Instead I usually see people obsessing more on the pile of details they insisted upon hearing, and this lessens their ability to rebuild trust. The outcome is no different in CNM relationships.

Honesty in relationships does not require telling every detail of every relationship to everyone. I do not recommend telling everyone about everything. Too much information (TMI) is full of unnecessary triggers and aspects of relations that do not have to be shared in order to be part of an honest agreement. How much to tell, when to tell, and whom to tell are challenges reported as frequently as is jealousy by CNM clients and research participants. Often clients don't see that too much disclosure is part of the jealousy problem; further, it may violate the privacy of other partners. One thing must be remembered: The "outside" partners are people, too. They have feelings and deserve privacy and respect. Some can share sex partners together, seeing and sharing all. Others have a low threshold for TMI and ought to limit what they actually see or hear. To the extent they do see or hear, when or if this triggers jealousy, specific tools such as self-talk and self-soothing need to be employed, as well as mindfulness (see Chapter 7) and calming techniques (just as in treating anxiety or negative thoughts).

Minimizing jealousy through careful, honest, but *considerate* sharing can be done. Figuring out how to do this in any given consensually nonmonogamous situation may be part of a larger, more complicated process.

Minimizing Jealousy for Couples

When there is a central or married couple, some general guidelines may be helpful. Regardless of how many partners the couple may have, their own relationship must have the necessary attention, care, and time. While it is often heard in CNM circles that "sex begets sex" (additional partners can spark the sex life of the married or central couple) outside partners are not a replacement for the solid footing of that original or central couple.

When a spouse or couple complains of jealous feelings or behavior, assess the couple's own relationship:

1. Find out how much time the couple is spending together alone. Are they dating each other? How is the married/primary couple's sex life when they do not have other partners?

2. What kinds of stressors and other issues are impacting their marriage or relationship and possibly the complaining partner's feelings?
3. Are they using the outside sex to avoid dealing with their own problems or sex life? If not, have the outside sex relationships overpowered their couple time, sex life, or family life?
4. Normalize changes in the couple's relationship. It's common, even expectable, for a long-term or primary couple to be less excited when together with each other, than they may be when with outside partners. Partners who have been together for a while are familiar with each other. Body and relational chemistries change from hunting and mating, to bonding and nesting chemicals. This does not mean that the primary partners love each other less! Just *differently.* This is part of the path of long-term relationships and why such partners need skills to maintain a mutually genuine intimate life. For some, this includes keeping sexy chemicals going by having sex with additional partners, but the couple must also focus on doing what is right for their own relationship at any given juncture.

If a couple has swinger partners or sexual playmates who do not live in, and who are not intended to be important love relationships, the couple may think jealousy won't occur. Both spouses may have fun with the play partners, then be surprised when either one of them reacts badly with upset feelings.

The Case of Kenny and Krista

Krista and Kenny illustrate several problems with and interventions for jealousy. They have known each other since high school, got married in their twenties, now are thirty-something parents. He was always a nonmonogamous person and did not try to pretend otherwise. When they married, Krista knew that CNM was part of the deal. She also enjoys sexual liaisons with additional partners and was a willing bride.

Kenny and Krista are neither swingers nor polyamorists, but they do practice expanded monogamy. They are an example of sharing *couple-friends-with-benefits.* They do know their additional partners well; these partners are usually friends, themselves married in open agreements. No one is in love with anyone other than their respective spouses (so they all report), each couple has their own lives. They all share some social activities together, and when schedules and desires coincide (not very frequently with several busy couples!), arrangements are made and everyone shares what they describe as fun sex parties.

Krista is as enthusiastic about these times as is her husband, and she often initiates them. Krista and the others usually drink during these dates. Even though Krista initiated the dates, sometimes when she sees Kenny with another female, she suddenly flips emotionally and says mean things, trying to ruin their evening. Other times Krista is fine and the evening goes well, but the next day she is upset and becomes angry with Kenny.

Through counseling we learned that some everyday needs of marriage for Krista are not being met. These unmet needs have nothing to do with outside partners or the generalized anxiety Krista has long struggled with. Feeling insecure because of marital issues and the generalized anxiety, Krista is, however, easily triggered into jealousy when she sees her husband give attention to someone else. Add alcohol and stir.

Kenny self-describes as having a very low jealousy level. He was not defensive in responses or demeanor during sessions when it was suggested that his behaviors might have something to do with Krista's difficulties. His goal is truly to help Krista and make this work. He suggested or accepted ideas of several ways he could be more supportive, demonstrative, and stay more connected with Krista. She started using skills that she had learned to calm anxiety, and to self-soothe when she did feel jealous.

Alcohol consumption was reduced on dates with friends. Krista agreed that Kenny should sometimes have sex with their female friend without Krista being there. She doesn't need to see everything that goes on and she, too, is "allowed" to see their male friend alone at times. These interventions proved helpful to their marriage. Also Kenny started spending more time with their children, responding to one of the complaints Krista expressed.

Krista experienced fewer triggers to jealousy when some were eliminated or minimized, underlying needs for connection in her own relationship were strengthened, and she used personal calming and positivity skills when she did get set off. Kenny also responded with more compassion and reassurance, once understanding the many contributors to Krista's upset feelings.

Some individuals and partners employ similar interventions but do not experience a lessening of jealousy. In these cases, two approaches may be necessary: assessing whether or not this person really wants CNM enough to delve deeply and do some uncomfortable personal work, or decide to opt out of consensual nonmonogamy. If a person truly wants to do the work, success in healing jealousy may be achieved, or at least jealousy may be reduced considerably to a manageable occurrence.

Use Techniques for Healing Jealousy

CNM requires that individuals face and examine jealousy. Like James, who cried and knew that his feelings had to do with fear and questioning his own value, anyone involved in honest multipartnering must be able to question what their jealousy is about, share deep feelings, allow themselves to be comforted, and let go of jealousy.

Healing jealousy may require acceptance that *jealousy is a feeling not necessarily based on current facts*. If jealousy is unmanageable, most likely it has a foundation in the person's past. Present-day events may trigger the feelings, but much more than what is going on today is contributing to that person's inability to get a handle on jealousy. Ability to become aware of and speak directly about underlying feelings has to be acquired, rather than essentially saying, *I feel jealous, so you stop doing that.*

Healing may involve:

- looking at past experience, including family of origin and prior relationships;
- dealing with fear of abandonment, loss, and being left out;
- psychosomatic trauma and PTSD healing techniques as applied to jealousy and the traumas underlying the person's jealousy;
- alternative and complementary therapies such as mindfulness, meridian tapping, hypnosis, Reiki, guided visualizations, acupuncture, EMDR, and others which may help according to individual response;
- separating past from present circumstances and changing behavior accordingly;
- grieving over the loss of being "the only one" this person loves and the idea that "being the only one creates security";
- creating bonding and security over the uniqueness and value of the relationship as it exists (part of more-than-one);
- examining and improving feelings about self;
- verifying (and discarding or making use of) what is believed others feel about, or how others view, the client;
- using thought-stopping and positive self-talk;
- learning anxiety relief approaches such as self-soothing and calming techniques, including mindfulness;
- honestly expressing pain and fears, using "I" language;
- accepting on a deep level soothing and reassurance from partners;
- learning or improving connection and sexual skills;
- learning compersion.

Teach Compersion as a Personal Development

Compersion is:

> A feeling of joy when a loved one invests in and takes pleasure from another romantic or sexual relationship. Commentary: Compersion can be thought of as the opposite of jealousy. Compersion is a positive emotional reaction to a loved one's other relationship. The term was coined by the Kerista Commune. It differs from candaulism in that compersion does not specifically refer to joy regarding the sexual activity of one's partner, but refers instead to joy at the relationship with another romantic or sexual partner. It is analogous to the feeling of joy a parent feels when their children marry or that best friends feel for each other when they are happy in a romantic relationship.
> "I feel compersion when I see my husband come home happy from spending time with his girlfriend. His happiness brings me happiness."
>
> (Joreth, 2010)

Barber and Julie, married over thirty years, illustrate compersion. Both spouses have had an outside lover off and on for most of their marriage. Each knows who the other's outside partner is. In an interview, Barber revealed that he plans nice things to do and say to Julie when he comes back from any date. Barber doesn't have much trouble with jealousy; Julie sometimes does, but both share a general feeling of compersion: They are genuinely happy for the joy the partner feels when sharing time with another. Barber states, and many consensually nonmonogamous people agree:

> Julie is giving me a gift, allowing me to see Luca. I mean, we both feel that if our spouse can enjoy pleasure and friendship with someone special, why would we want to stop that? We talk about things and we have our rules and limitations on it, but it's a gift. So I bring her back a present! We usually have a dinner or spend some alone time after one of us has a date with anyone else. I always make sure we reconnect with *us*, and I thank her for allowing me to do this.

Consensual nonmonogamy is a gift. When there are multiple partners, all of whom share meaningful relationships, like James, Jenna, and Martin, each relationship has integrity. James and Jenna are married; Martin is a secondary partner, not married. But they all live as significant others. Martin is respected and considered an equal partner. If he were to experience jealousy, he needs the same compassion and response as was given to James. As with Barber and Julie, compersion is a normal state for this couple. They are familiar with each other and with their respective other partners; all find joy in their shared situation. Compersion is the status quo.

We are certainly not socialized to feel compersion. Compersion is antithetical to how we view relationships and expect to operate in them. A common view is that we should get all our pleasure and happiness from a single partner *and* only experience it together with that partner. Even those CNM practitioners who have found their way to such positive feelings as compersion may be aware that their friends and relatives would consider them "crazy" for not only allowing, but enjoying the fact that a partner loves someone else as well.

June and Ben have a CNM marriage and three children. June relates that while she is glad that both she and Ben truly experience compersion, the feeling is also scary because she anticipates judgment from "the marriage police"—friends, relatives, and other parents at PTA meetings, school sporting events, and her local grocery store—if they knew about June and Ben's arrangement. This is one reason many people in CNM relationships hide their true lives. June exclaimed to me, "The marriage police would definitely disapprove of Ben having a lover and would pile even more disapproval on me for being happy about it, if they even could believe that I am happy about it!"

I have worked with monoamorous and polyamorous persons who wanted to feel compersion. In the case of Jill and Jack, Jack illustrates a form of compersion regarding his wife when he says he wishes his wife *would* have sex with someone else—someone she enjoys. When the sex dies down (or just dies), as is common in many otherwise good relationships, I have heard partners express wishes similar to Jack's. One partner sees the other's loss of interest in sex and perhaps rightfully senses that if this partner could experience joy in sex again that they would "wake up." Their sexuality would be revived. Reports from CNM practitioners, literature, and clinical experience confirm that such is true. Sparks for one partner can bring fire to the other partner as well. Swingers swing in part because of the positive result to the sex life of their primary relationship. Polyamorists know that loving more than one person can benefit all relationships, including sexually.

June, my client, explains that her experience with compersion started when her husband "woke up" sexually:

> The romance and sex life in our marriage were at an all-time low. We had financial stressors, responsibilities and schedules of three kids, and we both had to work; we had forgotten what it was like to have fun, to enjoy each other. I'm very serious when I say that I was happy to find out that my husband was still sexual at all. He talked about his date with Lin, a woman he'd met through a consulting job, I saw his face and his eyes look brighter than in a long time. His vitality re-emerged and I had not seen that in him or in our home for many years. He was actually excited about this new woman, about sex, about the work and fun he was sharing with Lin. I genuinely felt and told him, "I am so happy for you!"

Part of compersion is expressing appreciation for everyone involved. Even in the less-committed swinging and friendship CNM situations, the "outside" partners are people, too. They may not be part of daily life, everyone isn't in love, they don't live together. But sharing these intimate, pleasurable, fun, and exciting times together is a gift. I tell clients: *Treat everyone like a present! Express appreciation. Keep boundaries and communication clear.*

One of my female clients is considering being a "third" for an S and M couple who want a female playmate. This client, Sue, said she's cautious about getting involved with them because of how each of them spoke to her at one point. The woman told Sue that she didn't like that her partner had suggested a particular sex act to do with Sue because, the woman said, "That's OUR thing." When the husband heard how his wife felt, he cut Sue off from communication suddenly, after they'd all been texting for a few weeks and had met for coffee and conversation several times.

Sue's feelings were hurt, even though she's not in a romance with either person. Sue said to me:

> Most people don't want to be a "third." But a lot of couples want a female to play with. [I agreed that being a third is a tough position with risks.] Right?!? That's why I think people should treat thirds like a real gift!

Sue is showing how appreciation for every partner is a fundamental necessity. Everyone involved in CNM partnerships has feelings, is being brave sharing themselves and their partners in nontraditional formats. Whether partners are set up as equals or are considered seconds, thirds, "satellites," or outside partners, everyone can feel jealous and afraid at times. Regardless of what type or how many partners, all need to be able to manage jealousy through appropriate expression. All need to have feelings be received and answered. It's a lot of work for everyone!

Other interventions generally helpful in dealing with jealousy:

- Acknowledge everyone's feelings of fear, confusion, and bravery.
- Encourage everyone to show care, respect, and appreciation for themselves, and for everyone else in all their relationships.
- Teach communication skills.
- Teach calming skills, self-soothing, and self-talk.
- Teach use of visualization techniques.
- Recommend journaling.
- Teach mindfulness.

References

Joreth. (2010). Compersion. Available at: www.urbandictionary.com/define.php?term=Compersion

Merriam-Webster. Jealous. Retrieved April 10, 2017 from www.merriam-webster.com/dictionary/jealous

Orion, R. (2007). *Polyamory and the bisexual marriage*. Research report. San Francisco: Saybrook Graduate School and Research Center.

Orion, R. (2008). *From traditional to open marriage*. Case study report. San Francisco: Saybrook Graduate School & Research Center.

Orion, R. (2011). Examining definitions and treatments of low desire and low-sex marriage (Doctoral dissertation). Available from ProQuest Dissertations and Theses Global database (Dissertation No. 3465923).

Case Excerpt: Ann and Stan

Ann and Stan were clients who also volunteered to be interviewed for research on consensual nonmonogamy (CNM). Their change from traditional marriage to a *don't ask, don't tell* CNM arrangement was not successful. Ann and Stan were not studied longitudinally. Their case has been presented at scientific sexuality conferences alongside that of Jill and Jack to show contrast in situations and factors, which are discussed after their story.

Ann and Stan are each in their forties. Stan travels for his job in business; Ann is a consultant and author. Stan has two adult children from a previous marriage. Ann regularly practiced an Eastern religion prior to her marriage to Stan. Stan does not identify with any religion but espouses a practice of positive thinking and affirmations, thankfulness, and forgiveness.

Ann and Stan enjoyed an exciting sex life when they first met. They both express that the other has been a helpful partner in dealing with life issues, such as Stan's former alcoholism and Ann's depression. They have been married for 9 years.

Over time, Ann became more involved with her work and less involved intimately with her husband. Eventually she struggled to maintain any desire for sexual activities, which she claims were never a priority in her life, especially as someone who had espoused an ascetic Eastern lifestyle. Stan always had high sexual interest, and the couple tried many avenues to create an acceptable sex life to both of them, including medical testing and couples' workshops. Traditional approaches of sex therapy for "low sex" couples failed them. On the brink of divorce, they accepted the idea of trying an open sexual agreement.

Ann was leery at first, but she became excited about the idea when she learned she could not only make rules and boundaries about the situation, but also free herself from pressure. Stan was pleased about the idea but did not know how he would find partners, and he did not want to stop having sex with his wife. Ann agreed that the open arrangement would not end their own sex life. They planned date nights and practical changes to assure relaxed time together. For many months this worked well.

Stan complained, however, that he could not find outside partners that were acceptable within the parameters of his agreement with Ann. He decided to use the internet and pay what he called professionals, as long as they did not use drugs and followed strict safe sex practices. He said this was better than going crazy with no sex, and that some women were companionable. He still had sex with his wife. Therapy and their CNM plan helped, but after some months of making an effort to carve out time and be sexually expressive, Ann's enthusiasm waned. She then remained less than enthusiastic.

A comparatively sexless year passed for Ann and Stan, during which Ann had begun working 60 hours a week. Unaddressed problems came to a head. Stan claimed Ann had never consistently honored her part of the commitment by keeping their couple time sacred. He stated that she had a lover that used all her time: her work. One day their dog died unexpectedly, and Ann was very emotional. She reached out to Stan in a way that had been absent in their relationship for some time, after which they had particularly intimate and exciting sex. Ann then declared she wanted the monogamous agreement back in place to "keep our relationship in that space."

Stan did not want this, claiming Ann had become a workaholic, which she admitted was true, and that she had again become depressed. He had finally met someone he liked (not a sex worker) and did not wish to discard this possible relationship when Ann had not been keeping her commitments to him. He agreed, however, if she put time back into their lives, he would "close" the marriage again.

This distressed Ann and they saw their therapist. Ann agreed she was seriously overworking and becoming depressed. She now wanted to label Stan as a sex addict, however. When Stan next left for his weekly work schedule out of town, Ann stopped answering his calls and sent him an email with an ultimatum to close the marriage or get a divorce. Stan chose to move forward with a new relationship. Ann did not continue counseling for her depression or overworking.

Stan did not regret the open relationship and felt it helped his marriage when Ann was also following the plan. They both stated they would have divorced sooner and even less amicably if they had not tried it.

Discussion: Why Did CNM Not Work for This Couple?

- They tried expanded monogamy as a last ditch effort to heal a marriage already in crisis because of mental health reasons and differing desire levels.
- Ann did not keep to the agreements mutually designed with Stan.
- Ann did not get help with her issues involving overwork and depression. These issues impacted their relationship negatively, regardless of their sex life. CNM addressed only the desire discrepancy and could work only when both partners adhered to their mutual agreements.
- Ann was confused by the close sex she and Stan experienced after their dog died. She mistakenly thought this meant that if she and Stan were exclusive again, that this level of emotional intensity and ease of sexual connection would remain. "Grief sex" is a known phenomenon, however. Deep emotional sharing is part of connected sex. Events such as loss or divorce can often create a temporary state of shared sadness and memories. This is not an indication that the relationship could be successfully reinstated.

- Ann assumed the sexual arrangements would make or break their partnership and did not give equal weight to her own mental and physical health issues. She was also not able to follow either a monogamous or a nonmonogamous agreement. That's not her fault, nor Stan's—fault is not the issue—but their differing desire levels remained facts that neither could change.

6 Communication Issues of Honesty and Disclosure

"Social change happens when deeply felt private experiences are given public legitimacy" (commonly attributed to Mahatma Gandhi). Unfortunately, the deeply held private experience of loving intimately more than one partner at a time is a risky one to disclose socially, impeding public legitimacy. Talking within and outside of consensually nonmonogamous relationships is a multi-faceted matter.

"Communicate, communicate, communicate!" declared Jack, a research participant (Orion, 2008a, 2011) when asked what advice he would give to others trying consensual nonmonogamy (CNM). My 17 years of working with CNM clients, reading, and conducting research on polyamory and other forms of CNM clarify that a lot of communication is required to make this lifeway and lovestyle work.

Therapists are trained in helping partners learn specific communication skills, be it compassionate listening, "I" language, showing appreciation, response versus reaction, and a myriad of other approaches. What are CNM partners communicating about which is different from what other clients need to discuss in therapy? This chapter is not about *how* to communicate, but *what* to communicate and what to disclose. How much, and what is discussed between partners about other partners? How much, and what, about the CNM situation is shared with the outside world? These matters are not issues in monogamy. These topics, involving focused communication and negotiation in CNM, are examined:

- Interrelationship negotiation and disclosure:

    o How much sexual and emotional disclosure between partners is desirable?
    o Visibility vs. invisibility.

- Disclosure beyond the relationships:

    o A closet keeps things safe but is a small space.
    o Disclosure in public.

Interrelationship Negotiation and Disclosure

Emotional safety requires each partner to have a certain level of self-esteem, skills in communicating needs and about practical issues, and the ability to compromise and share. For each partner to feel essentially secure, a comfortable level of interrelationship disclosure must be negotiated.

How Much Sexual and Emotional Disclosure about Partners Is Desirable?

How much is too much information? Honesty is a core value of consensual nonmonogamy, so what partners tell each other is of paramount importance to making CNM relationships work. Some partners want to know as much as possible about their partners' other partners and what they all do together; others want to know as little as possible. What works for any set of partners is part of what they must figure out and may be an issue to be addressed in therapy.

If partners want high disclosure and detailed consent, they may need help discussing issues that are not common to therapy offices in which all relationships treated are monogamous. CNM partners must discuss what type of sex is acceptable, with whom, and under what circumstances. When partners engage sexually with others, is it with or without genital contact or penetration? With what gender(s)? Does it have to be anonymous? Can liaisons be shared together with known or committed partners only? Must partners be casual, or is bonding acceptable? How frequently can partners meet? Is "kinky" sex acceptable (see Chapter 9)? Must existing partners meet new prospects before sexual activity occurs? Does anyone have veto power with regard to a partner's choice of another? If so, by what reasoning, and how is this carried out?

Something monogamous couples never need to discuss are the ways partners can be involved in their belongings and personal space. Examples I've heard stated in my office are: "No, I don't want your lover wearing my flip flops to the pool," or "It's OK if you and he make love in the guest room but not in our bed." Such questions and issues may require clinically facilitated communication and negotiation, but agreements are as individual as each set of relationships and the persons in them.

Communication and negotiation are foundational elements in maintaining honesty and trust, both necessary for emotional safety. Couples ought not to attempt CNM unless their own relationship is stable and partners communicate well. Building this foundation takes time, cannot be rushed, and needs to take place at "an appropriate pace . . . the more deeply you trust someone, the easier it will be to take the leap of faith as you explore the possibilities beyond monogamy" (cited in Gerard & Brownlee, 2015). As CNM relationships often happen whether or not individuals or partners are thus prepared, those who wish to succeed in CNM may consult a therapist with the need to learn skills for open communication.

Visibility vs. Invisibility

Visibility is a word used in some CNM partnerships to describe agreements that support transparency in all aspects of the additional or outside relationship(s)—a no secrets policy. Everyone tells everyone else about everything. *Invisibility* refers to agreements that allow for some measure of autonomy and privacy within and among relationships.

Personally and professionally I have seen more problems when too much information is shared, than when limits are placed on the sharing of details. Each person and each relationship needs their own boundaries and private space, mentally and physically. Everyone has a right to privacy, and to their own head issues. Partners who share a lot of details about others can be destructive, even if they are relatively well-meaning about their conversations. There's a fine line between honest sharing and negotiation, and telling too much information to too many people.

Finding that line between how much to tell and what to keep private can be tricky. Individuals vary in what they can handle, in what they think they want to know, and in their abilities to keep their mouth shut. The reasoning I have heard from clients for disclosing everything is that they feel it is dishonest not to do so. *Honest* is one of those words that is not defined or carried out the same by everyone. Disclosure is also about the other person(s) not feeling left out. A partner may want to know more but cannot handle what they hear. Fundamental is the self-esteem level of each person.

Angie, Jan, and Chad are a good example. Angie and Jan are partners who both fell in love with Chad. The women asked Chad to move in with them. Jan explains:

> We started out thinking the best policy is to tell each other everything—who sleeps with who, when; even what sexual activities we shared with each person, every feeling we all had. I thought I'd feel less jealous if I knew it all. Ha! It turned into these long discussions with a lot of crying. Instead of feeling better, I felt even more excluded and I couldn't get the images out of my mind of Chad and Angie together.

Angie chimes in: "I felt like I had no privacy! I ended up thinking of Jan whenever Chad and I were together."

Jan looks at Angie and says in a tone indicating she was sorry:

> I didn't want that, I really didn't. We had to learn what we could share without crossing certain lines. Full honesty does not mean every personal and sexual detail and feeling have to be told. I used to think so and maybe that works for some people. We may not be perfect but we figured out a balance of what's OK to keep to ourselves.

Angie adds:

> There's less drama and upset, and I feel more secure, not less. You just have to accept that each relationship has its own way and space and allow that to be. I focus on my own time with Chad, not Jan's.

I've also heard clients describe a deep sense of belonging and intimacy among all partners when they do share all emotions and even what various partners do sexually with each other. These types of partners have reported to me a strong sense of self-confidence and do not question their place in the respective relationships; they report rarely experiencing jealousy throughout life, thus hearing intimate details is not usually disturbing. In my experience, such partnerships are less common in CNM than are those in which partners need to find a balance between disclosure and privacy.

Taormino (2008) states, "Trust is built in open relationships when [partners] are able to let one another know about their needs, decide together how to meet these needs, and then honor the agreement throughout relationships." Achieving this may take ongoing communication and re- evaluation about needs and behaviors that carry out agreements. As stated in Gerard and Brownlee (2015):

> This includes the ability to talk openly and honestly about attraction, feelings and relationships with secondary partners, a skill that is rarely easy for any couple. Many [partners] struggle with how to balance secrecy and privacy, as well as honesty versus over-sharing of information. [Partners] may come in with the expectation of equally open communication, when one . . . is more prone to autonomy and privacy by nature. Addressing jealousy, dispersion of time spent with co-marital partners, and agreement violation are examples of core issues that depend on open communication patterns. The . . . therapist must navigate [these] communication patterns, including frequent topics of discussion, partner perceptions, rule violations, and the [partners'] failure to communicate [effectively].

Each person must guide and inform the development of rules and boundaries around the issue of disclosure. I have found three elements to be a good basis for many CNM partners in deciding how much to say, to whom, within the partnerships: limit shared information to safety, scheduling, and minimal details about intimacy. If some partners can handle or benefit from more disclosure about sex and intimacy, then that's what works for them.

For CNM communication and disclosure issues within partnerships, the following may help:

- Everyone needs mindfulness practices (see Chapter 8), which help with centering and calm as well as with personal clarity about feelings of security and anxiety.
- Partners need to keep an eye out for each other. If someone seems to feel sad or bad, find out why. If it has to do with relationship security, be reassuring. Examine if rules, boundaries, and personal behaviors triggered a problem. (If this happens all the time, no matter what is done, the issue needs further examination.)
- Communicate, communicate, communicate. If something isn't working, partners must discuss it. If feelings come up, do not let things fester. Have

regular talks and schedule partner or family meetings to keep feelings heard and arrangements on track.

- Support all partners' emotional security by developing and maintaining workable boundaries of information disclosure between partners.
- Keep intimate aspects of each relationship TO that relationship. Unless sharing more is successful!
- Do not discuss issues about partner A with partner B. Especially if you have not first discussed them with partner A!

Disclosure Beyond Relationships

Who can know (and how much) about the CNM couple, partnership, group, or family? Because consequences can be serious, whether to be *open about being open* is an important topic for clinicians to understand. Risks, stressors, and benefits of "coming out poly" are discussed here, but in sessions therapists may also need to help clarify some variables. When it is safer (or for whatever reasons) for CNM partners to choose not to come out, help is needed managing challenges and difficulties caused by living secretively.

If partners choose to be publicly open, even with limitations, how do clients disclose their lifeway or lovestyle and deal with associated stressors? Under what circumstances does any type of disclosure take place, and at what stage of the relationship(s)? Answers to these questions are impacted by the social and political climate where partners live, who is involved in the partnership, group, or family, the careers of adults and school experiences of children, the condition and types of families of origin of each partner, and probably more factors.

A Closet Keeps Things Safe, But Is a Small Space

To tell, or not to tell, that is the question. That those in consensual nonmonogamy are at legal risk, including custody battles based on one parent being openly polyamorous, has been established (Cloud, 1999; Emens, 2004; Henrich & Trawinski, 2016; Johnson, n.d.; Orion, 2008a, 2011). That any form of nonmonogamy can be misunderstood and badly viewed if discovered is common knowledge among the population of CNM practitioners. Being open about CNM is a risk even in what is considered a safe environment, such as therapy (Emens, 2004; Haupert, Gesselman, Moors, Fisher, & Garcia, 2016; Henrich & Trawinski, 2016; Johnson, n.d.; Orion, 2007, 2008a, 2008b, 2011; Sheff, 2014; Weitzman, 1999, 2006).

Drescher (2004) illustrates the similarities faced by those in CNM lifeways to the dangers and benefits of coming out for LGBTQIQ persons with this reprint of a research excerpt, stating that the text remains true and can be unchanged except for the persons described (exchange "homosexual" or "gay" for "polyamorous" or "CNM"):

> Given the social stigma, the severity of antihomosexual [change to monogamy-centric] attitudes in the culture and the difficulties associated

with revealing one's sexual identity, why would a gay [poly] person come out at all? "Most frequently coming out involves choices about how to handle moments of ordinary daily conversation" (Magee and Miller, 1995). [On the positive side] coming out offers gay [CNM] people the possibility of integrating a wider range of previously split off affects, not just their sexual feelings . . . greater ease in expressing themselves, both to themselves and to others, can lead to an enormous enrichment of their work and relationships. To many, such activities constitute a reasonable definition of mental health.

Therapists need to be aware of the benefits to clients' mental and physical health of the coming out process and school themselves on methods and practices for assisting clients to navigate that process successfully.

For those who do not choose to come out as consensual nonmonogamists, maintaining the lifestyle secretly is possible, but may fail. Two of my research participants (2008a, 2011), Jack and his wife, Jill, kept their CNM agreement to themselves for years and did not see anyone in their home town as extramarital partners. Eventually, however, some of Jill's and Jack's friends discovered their arrangement. Jill and Jack had already been together and making CNM work for years before anyone found out. No one had noticed anything amiss about the marriage or the solid friendship shared by this couple. They were great parents and had been able to stay married and happily with their child in the same house years longer than they would have if they had not expanded their marriage sexually.

In counseling with me, they discussed how to respond to these critical friends and still maintain their open relationship. That Jack's work takes him out of town frequently, where he maintained his extramarital relationships, helped this couple keep a successful and relatively hidden CNM relationship for 27 years as of this writing. Friends stopped saying anything, and their now college-age son has never known about his parents' arrangement.

Jill and Jack experienced one example of social derision when CNM is "outed." Other of my respondents and clients have reported worse consequences such as loss of jobs, law suits with in-laws and extended family trying to take children away, bullying of children in school, loss of friends and family members, and other serious life consequences when "outsiders" know about CNM arrangements.

Many in polyamorous families want children to have an open model for relationships, and prefer not to teach children to keep secrets. Concerns for children's safety and social experience, however, may outweigh the desire to impart new positive values.

In 2009, the following was published from a research and literature review by Weitzman, Davidson, Phillips, Fleckenstein, and Morotti-Meeker:

> While 75% of polyamorous survey respondents wanted their children to know of their lifestyle, only 21% had actually informed their children of the full extent of their involvements with other partners. Some incorporate their

children with them in the company of their secondary partners, and indicate that they enjoy the process of modeling an alternative for their children. Other parents feel that sharing the news of their lifestyle would be too upsetting for their children, or would not be understood, or would be shared openly with neighbors and school friends. A survey of polyamorous individuals showed that nearly two decades later, 45% still were not "out" to their own children.

Though there is community and a growing population for all forms of CNM— online communities, in person meet-ups, sex clubs for swingers, and more— social acceptance and legal safety have not been established. Because of this fact, disclosure is a serious topic for CNM practitioners, and clinicians must be aware that "coming out poly"—or managing the stress of remaining closeted—is part of why clients may come for help. Similar to disclosing a sexual orientation, both secrecy and being open have drawbacks, challenges, and risks. Unfortunately at this time (2017 in the United States), effects on physical safety, careers, social status, and acceptance by family and friends must be considered when discussing living openly a consensually nonmonogamous lifeway and lovestyle.

Debra Anapol (2010), one of the first published authorities on consensual non-monogamy, discusses how social sanctions keep safely out of sight couples who are in successful CNM relationships, and who would potentially be good role models. I've seen this demonstrated through work with several group and open marriages of highly functional partners who have kept their relationships private to protect important and successful work they were doing, including ministry, social work, and running youth programs. They did not want to risk their ability to help others by exposing themselves to criticism of their preferred lovestyle.

Disclosure in Public

Some clients have disclosed their CNM situation to one individual whom they believe is agreeable and trustworthy, only to find that someone else overheard the conversation, or was later told by that trusted friend. The unintended recipient of information may not be "cool" with CNM and may cause problems.

"This is my partner Tom, and my other partner Jake." Unless at a designated CNM "meet-up" or gathering, it may not be wise to introduce partners in this honest way. A major stressor of remaining closeted is that some partners cannot act or be treated as partners except in private.

Hiding multiple partnerships in public may be safer but can cause hurt feelings and requires discussion between partners. There are many stressors resulting from keeping important secrets such as sexual orientation and alternative lifeways or lovestyles, for which CNM partners may seek clinical support. These include (Browning, Reynolds, & Dworkin, 1991):

- Fear of being discovered and shunned (or worse).
- If children are in the situation, partners may be forced to meet away from home.

- Emotional distress or mental health issues caused by forced lack of recognition of one's true self and of one's partners.

Sarah, a CNM client, told me:

> I always felt like the third wheel, like I was a less important partner. Hiding and lying about ourselves made us all feel that we were doing something wrong by loving each other, even though we know it isn't. I'm not sure what we should do about it, it's more than awkward to just be open about who we are. But Tom and Nancy are married, everyone knows them, they don't have to hide their feelings for each other, but they have to hide me. Like I'm just some pitiful, single friend always hanging around them.

Partners need help deciding what is said to whom about their relationships, how partners are introduced to others, who can show affection to whom, and in what situations. I don't think there are pat answers to these questions. Factors must be taken into account such as where partners live, attitudes of family members and friends, occupations of partners, and whether there are children. Which (if any) family members can know about the CNM and how much? Can children be told the truth? To this last question especially there are many potential issues to be discussed, which are further explored in Chapter 10.

Before gay marriage was legal, there was the option of drawing up papers addressing medical decisions, estate dissolution, trust funds, and other marriage and family contracts. Consensual nonmonogamy partners who wish to create commitment ceremonies accompanied by privacy-protected legal documents have the right to do so. Some protections and benefits legally afforded married couples can be set up with different documents for CNM partners and families. Even a type of prenuptial agreement can be created. A CNM-friendly lawyer would have to be located and the contents of such contracts could be topics clarified with a therapist.

References

Anapol, D. (2010). *Polyamory in the 21st century: Love and intimacy with multiple partners.* Lanham, MD: Rowman & Littlefield.

Browning, C., Reynolds, A. L., & Dworkin, S. H. (1991). Affirmative psychotherapy for lesbian women. *Counseling Psychologist, 19* (2), 177–196.

Cloud, J. (1999, November 15). Henry & Mary & Janet & . . . Is your marriage a little dull? The "polyamorists" say there's another way. *Time, 154* (20), 90–91.

Drescher, J. (2004). The closet: Psychological issues of being in and coming out. *Psychiatric Times 21* (12).

Emens, E. F. (2004). Monogamy's law: Compulsory monogamy and polyamorous existence. *NYU Review of Law and Social Change, 29,* 277–376.

Gerard, A. & Brownlee, A. (2015). Assessment guidelines and clinical implications for therapists working with couples in sexually open marriages. *Sexual and Relationship Therapy, 30* (4), 462–474.

Haupert, M., Gesselman, A., Moors, A., Fisher, H., & Garcia, J. (2016). Prevalence of experiences with consensual non-monogamous relationships: Findings from two nationally representative samples of single Americans, *Journal of Sex & Marital Therapy*, doi: 10.1080/0092623X.2016.1178675.

Henrich, R., & Trawinski, C. (2016). Social and relationship challenges facing polyamorous clients. *Sexual and Relationship Therapy*. Available at: http:/dx.doi.org/10.1080/148681994.2016.117.4331

Johnson, A. L. (n.d). Counseling the polyamorous client: Implications for competent practice. Article 50. Retrieved May 16, 2017 from VISTAS Online, American Counseling Association professional library. www.counseling.org/library

Orion, R. (2007). *Polyamory and the bisexual marriage*. Research report. San Francisco: Saybrook Graduate School and Research Center.

Orion, R. (2008a). *From traditional to open marriage*. Case study report. San Francisco: Saybrook Graduate School & Research Center.

Orion, R. (2008b). Polyamory as treatment for low desire. Paper presented at the Western Regional Conference of the Society for the Scientific Study of Sexuality, April, 2008, San Diego, CA.

Orion, R. (2011). Examining definitions and treatments of low desire and low-sex marriage (Doctoral dissertation). Available from ProQuest Dissertations and Theses Global database (Dissertation No. 3465923).

Sheff, E. A. (2014). *The polyamorists next door: Inside multiple relationships and families.* Lanham, MD: Rowman & Littlefield.

Taormino, T. (2008). *Opening up: A guide to creating and sustaining open relationships.* San Francisco: Cleis Press.

Weitzman, G. D. (1999). What psychology professionals should know about polyamory: The lifestyles and mental health concerns of polyamorous individuals. Paper presented at 8th Annual Diversity Conference, Albany, NY, March.

Weitzman, G. D. (2006). Therapy with clients who are bisexual and polyamorous. *Journal of Bisexuality*, 6(1–2), 137–164, doi: 10.1300/J159v06n01_08.

Weitzman, G. D., Davidson, J., Phillips, R., Fleckenstein, J., & Morotti-Meeker, C. (2009). What psychology professionals should know about polyamory. National Coalition for Sexual Freedom. Baltimore, MD. Available at: http://instituteforsexuality.com/wp-content/uploads/2014/05/what-therapists-should-know-about-Polyamory-1.pdf

Case Excerpt: Sandra, Matt, and Jon

Sandra consulted me about her marriage with Matt when the relationship got complicated: both spouses had fallen in love with Jon. Over a period of months each individual had sessions alone, Matt and Sandra had couples sessions together, and all three partners had triad sessions. Each claims that the time in life they spent as a triad was beautiful, very important, and led to other changes—not all of which each liked. This trio did not make it in the long term, but their story illustrates many issues in polyamory.

Matt and Sandra live in an upper-middle-class neighborhood. Each has a college degree. Matt is an engineer and Sandra is a professor. Matt identifies as bisexual. Sandra is heterosexual but considers herself open. They have been together as a couple for 15 years, 10 of which they have been married. Neither had married previously, but both have had long-term relationships. They got married because they loved each other and wanted a family. They had a traditionally monogamous agreement. They do want children but have been putting this off for a variety of reasons. Sandra is in her late thirties and is starting to feel her biological clock run out.

Like Matt, Jon is in his early forties. He is a health professional. He and his wife have two daughters. Matt and Sandra, and Jon and his wife, have been casual friends since Jon and Matt met at a home building store. Jon identifies as bisexual and states he had never experienced gay sex prior to falling in love with Matt.

All three of these partners were compelled into a polyamorous agreement: Matt and Jon fell in love with each other; Sandra wanted to stay married and accept her husband's bisexuality. After Matt and Jon had been seriously involved for a few months, Jon disclosed his orientation to his wife, who is not open like Sandra. Jon's wife filed for divorce and banned him from the house. She threatened to keep their girls from Jon, but he managed to negotiate with her to maintain regular visits. Eventually a divorce settlement was reached that includes joint custody.

Sandra reports, "I couldn't have done what Jon's wife did—kick her husband out." Matt became aware of his bisexuality only after being married for a few years; he had started having periodic relations with men that were not ongoing. He did not immediately disclose his bisexual orientation to his wife, but once he did, he was honest with her each time he was involved with another person. Matt had been married to Sandra for about seven years when he met Jon for the first time; unlike the others, this developed into a serious relationship. He told Sandra about the depth of his relationship with Jon after the two had been involved for 2 months. This and other issues, such as family planning and Sandra's depression, led them to seek counseling.

In counseling, Matt and Sandra officially accepted the fact of Matt's bisexuality—that this is not something Matt could stop or control. They also reiterated their love for and commitment to one another. Matt stated, "I can't imagine life without Sandra, I am distraught that I've caused her this pain." Sandra was troubled by the time passing before having children. She related, "I was so afraid that Matt's relationship with Jon would take away from our marriage. I wanted to accept Matt's bisexuality but I didn't want to feel left out." Sandra liked and was attracted to Jon. She and Jon started spending time together, which soon included sex (with Matt's consent). Sandra eventually suggested a three-way equal "marriage" in which they both had someone else to love.

Matt reports, "That was an amazing and beautiful time and something unexpected, because that wasn't an idea I'd had in my head. It just happened and we all agreed. We tried it and it was great for over a year."

Jon had married his wife because he loved her and wanted to have a family.

> Then I met Matt. We had a relationship, and he was married, too, but his wife became OK with us being together. I fell in love with Matt. It was unexpected; we met randomly at Home Depot! Later we decided to meet each other's wife. That wasn't a very good idea on my end. We were all friends until Carla learned I was bisexual. I ended up getting divorced, even though I still loved my wife, and I almost lost the kids. But Matt's wife, Sandra, wanted to include me in their relationship. So there I was in this unusual situation.

Jon says he loved two people at the same time when he was in the triad. He found Sandra different from any woman he had known. He "learned from her, cared about, and loved her." Matt and Sandra each loved two people at once, declaring they couldn't imagine life without one another, and each loved Jon. Matt states, "I want to be with Sandra the rest of my life, and it's a different kind of love than I feel for Jon," with whom he also feels a deep connection not replaced by other relationships.

Matt and Sandra talk about their marriage as their primary relationship, with Jon as a secondary partner to both of them. They do not necessarily use this language, and over time each reveals slightly different interpretations and feelings. They all state that they had not heard the term *polyamory* until I introduced them to the idea as an honest way of having an open relationship to incorporate Matt's bisexuality into his marriage with Sandra. Jon said, "I did feel it was a primary-secondary set-up, I often felt like a third wheel."

Sandra and Jon spent significant time alone together on weekends when Matt's work took him out of town. Jon and Matt continued to share time together away from Sandra. The three also spent time together, never moving into the same house, but discussing the possibility of investing in a shared home in the future. All were concerned with secrecy to protect Jon's access to his children, who never knew about Matt and Sandra.

Matt describes:

> I did feel love for both people, coincidentally of different sexes, and while I was married. I hadn't imagined myself like that, but for whatever reason that's how it was. Sometimes I felt really entangled. When I woke up some mornings I had the sense that these two minds were going inside me and they were so wrapped up in each other. I was trying to unwind them just to see what was there. Part of me is like "Oh, my God, I'm 41. Now this is happening?"
>
> I was at a wedding last night. This eighty-something-year-old couple comes out of their hotel room. They're arm-in-arm, they're so adorable, they just had the biggest grins and they were amazing. It's what I want—to grow old with Sandra. Even she can see that we can't help loving Jon.

While Matt, Sandra, and Jon were living as a triad, all reported communicating about everything and being generally honest. In sessions, however, individual partners revealed that the men as a couple did not share everything with Sandra, nor did the triad present themselves openly in public or to friends, which could have jeopardized them all professionally, among other risks. Sandra did not disclose all her thoughts and feelings to both men, nor for a time, to me in counseling. Many things did bother her about the three-way relationship, and other issues in her life built up, but she didn't disclose them so these issues were never addressed. This gave the men the idea that everything was fine with her for longer than it really was. The private relationship of Matt and Jon did cause stress for Sandra, but Matt and Jon stated that she did not get help with her feelings and that they did not discuss these problems together as a triad.

Sandra did say, "I wanted to make my relationship with Jon equal to Matt's relationship with Jon, with my marriage still number one." As Sandra realized over time that it wasn't a perfectly balanced relationship, that Matt and Jon might have something different or deeper than she had with Matt, she became angry and started blaming Matt for his inability to control his impulses with men. She decided to move out. Matt was devastated. He believed that when hurt, Sandra blamed Matt's orientation, but factors other than his sexuality contributed heavily to Sandra's unhappiness. Matt stated that her depression was triggered by not getting help with changes in the relationships, the continued delay in having children (she had problems conceiving), and that she'd lost a job she had liked.

Matt says he feels that Sandra did a lot of things to avoid jealousy, or to help herself deal with it, but they didn't discuss it as a group to know how to help her. "And," he continues:

> Jon and I, we're good at hiding. Because we hid a part of ourselves for so long. Maybe we wanted, or felt like we wanted to do more together, but we

kind of hid it from Sandra; we didn't want her to think we had more than the three of us were sharing. I just felt really split in the middle. And I felt it the whole time. It was exciting because it was new, and I think each of them responded to me in a different way. But I wasn't really jealous of either one. I just wanted it to all be balanced. How do you measure and balance love? Each relationship—we just loved each other how we did, I don't think there's a control to turn up or down.

After Sandra moved out, Matt and Jon remained lovers for a time but decided to just remain friends when the stress of changes in the relationships made it difficult for them to be happy together. Jon can't say he'll never be involved with another man, but he does wish to be a husband and father. Jon disclosed to practically no one his sexual orientation nor his arrangement with Matt and Sandra for fear of losing his children and the respect of his conservative family.

Only my closest friends know. I'm protecting my child and my family. [His country of origin] is a more conservative society. I have a new girlfriend now, and I didn't tell her about my time with Matt and Sandra or my interest in men. Right now, I'm happy. I can't guarantee that that part of me will stay off, but right now I'm OK [with how things are]. When I was with them, we couldn't tell the whole truth, they told some people that I was only involved with Matt. And then I wouldn't feel like talking to those people again. They thought I was always with him, and the relationship wasn't like that at all. But it seemed like those few people who noticed something going on could more easily accept that Matt and I are bisexual than that all three of us loved each other.

Because of this half-truth being told, Matt and Sandra's friends later viewed problems with their marriage as being caused by Jon and Matt—that Jon had "taken Matt away" from Sandra. Sandra eventually wanted her marriage to appear that it had remained intact and usual, except that she had a bisexual husband. Sandra reports that having a bisexual husband caused less social stigma among friends than admitting to a love triad.

Jon now accepts himself as bisexual, but is not comfortable with the ramifications of that identity in society, nor for his future as a family man or professional. He says, "A huge negative is other people—is society—and the price I have paid for finding this out about myself."

Jon reports:

Sexually it was a very pure link between the three of us. It was the best sex I ever had. We were friends, we talked a lot, that was great. [A negative is that] later Sandra regretted a lot. I think she was really hurt. She felt let down when Matt and I were doing it [without her]. But she never said anything about it until much later. She was really happy at the time. I don't regret it. It was an experience and, you know, we loved each other a lot. I wouldn't change it.

Matt reports that for him there were positives and negatives:

> Hurt feelings, jealousy, and, yeah, possibly leading to break-up. Positives
> were true emotional connection and a lot of really high, beautiful sex. I
> didn't think Sandra would be so open but it was incredible while it was work-
> ing. She even suggested it first. But I think not knowing fully how to make
> this work, it's kind of like, we both needed to check in with each other a lot
> more . . . it all happened very fast.

Jon advises others:

> Just be very honest about what you feel about the other people. Like for me,
> I wasn't very honest and I never told Sandra my feelings or ones that were
> for him, not for her. But over time, you can't pretend. Over time she sensed
> that. She even said, "It's OK, it's like a perfect triangle: he's in love with
> you, you're in love with me, and I'm in love with him." But you know, no,
> it didn't work like that.

Matt advises:

> Try to know what you want, and why you want to do it. You have to know
> how it can work for you. Know what your goals are in having this kind of
> relationship. A lot of communication. A negative is the question, is it sustain-
> able? I don't know if we can answer that.

Matt had been an actively bisexual spouse for many years, but what they all consider the *profound relationship* of their triad lasted just over a year. Each participant described it as wonderful in many ways and something they would not give
up were they to go back and make choices again. At the time, Sandra suggested
having a commitment ceremony to include Jon in a kind of multiple marriage,
and she declared that should she become pregnant, it didn't matter to her which
man was the father. Each of them described this time as a personal, spiritual, and
sexual highlight of their lives.

Matt clarifies why he thinks the triad didn't sustain over time:

> I think for Sandra it was this last desperate hope of something, for salvaging
> things. And then everything shifted so quickly. She even says now she felt at
> that time like she was on such a euphoric high from it, like really physically
> and emotionally it was so elevating. But that didn't sustain, it came crashing
> down and that helped to bring her into her depression. That's what triggered
> the spiral. I think it's a combination of that, and she had to switch jobs.
> There were a lot of big changes at once.

Sandra adds:

> Don't get me wrong about all this either, because I don't regret sleeping with Jon, and I normally have lots of regrets. You know I was talking to Matt a couple weeks ago after we were separated and I was just saying, the time when I met Matt was one of the happiest times in my life. And another one was when the three of us were together. It was fantastic. It just didn't last long enough.

Jon's professional location changed to a more distant one, which took a toll on his and Matt's friendship. They felt guilty about Sandra. Matt remains open but has not been in a relationship with either a man or a woman 2 years after Sandra moved out. He still grieves over losing both his marriage to Sandra (with whom he remains in touch) and his lover.

Matt concludes:

> I saw this movie where the guy just said: "Look, I will always be there. I will be loyal to the end. But I will not be faithful." And that's how I feel. I don't understand that part of me—and I've lost both people I love because they can't make peace with it either. Sandra's gone and it kills me. I have these amazing dreams about my attachment to her, and my love, and they're sensual. It's overpowering. So that's extremely confusing for me. They were complicated relationships and there's no guide book. To do anything different, it's like, people are kind of floundering.

7   It's About Time

Introduction

"In a family, love is spelled T I M E" (anonymous, inspired by Dieter F. Uchtdorf). Everyone has the same amount of time. Not all have the same number of relationships. The busy single person often feels there's never enough time. Traditional couples can be overwhelmed with life's demands and pass like ships in the night. Add children, and the couple may feel like roommates and parents, with little or no time for intimacy or romance. Now add more adult relationships, and quality time is beyond stretched. Partners who make consensual nonmonogamy (CNM) work include time management and scheduling when designing their arrangements.

Problems with time may involve many issues which often overlap. Sorting these out means untangling balls of intertwined problems, events, people, emotions, and behaviors. To the extent that we clinicians can isolate where *time management* is a catalyst for problems, we work to find practical solutions.

Concerns of CNM partners include:

- making time for everyone;
- compromising and prioritizing;
- the quality of shared time.

Making Time for Everyone

Ongoing scheduling conversations can lead to drama, with feelings of being left out or chosen over. Established routines help all involved know what's going on and what to expect. Routines have to be somewhat flexible, but knowing when needs will be met according to a schedule avoids continuous conversations about who gets time now. Partners feel more emotionally secure (and the house may run more smoothly!) when each person knows when their own needs will be met. It's easier to make plans while feeling secure in relationships and all know that their turn is coming.

Clinicians can help clients create manageable and realistic schedules reflecting each partner's needs. Once agreements are made, each partner must follow through. When changes need to be made, help partners discuss and adjust time agreements.

Some CNM situations have equal sharing time with all partners. Others have time allotments that reflect, in part, the importance or place of each relationship in the group, sometimes referred to as a "polyhierarchy."

Consensual Nonmonogamy Formats

For ease of discussion, I am using the term *primary, seconds,* and so on, as more efficient than "one partner's other partner" and the like. Many in CNM do not use these or any term indicating place or roles.

CNM formats with primaries, seconds, or thirds may include:

- fully committed polyamorous partners, groups, and families;
- couple swingers with secondary partners whom they don't see again;
- couples open to additional partners who are trusted friends;
- couples open to various arrangements with known or new partners;
- couples with one bisexual or queer spouse who sees same-sex or queer secondary partners;
- partners with special circumstances, such as one spouse being disabled and allowing the partner to relate to others;
- partners who have a specific sexual interest not shared by one partner, but is shared with another.

In any of these situations, seconds may be cared about long term, or may be seen once and never again. In any of these situations, a partner may be triggered into jealousy if feelings arise of not getting enough time with someone, or if agreed-upon time arrangements are not followed. If extra-relationship parity is lacking— one partner does not have a secondary but the other does, or one partner has more time with their second—emotions, including jealousy, may arise.

These issues are difficult for primary partners. Being a second or third partner can also be fraught with emotion, however, especially when the secondary partner has no other relationship (i.e., they are *only* a second or third to a couple or individual, but have no personal primary relationship). There's a risk that the second and one primary become more involved than planned, a situation I have seen in my office many times. Secondary partners may also become more attached than desired, or need more time with another partner than was originally planned for or expected.

James, Martin, and Jenna call themselves a throuple. James and Jenna have been married for 18 years and had other partners prior to Martin. Jenna explains:

> We've had other partners but not everyone works out. We don't feel like another love is less important, but Martin doesn't live here. We all see each other nearly every day though, and we do a lot of things together as a three-some. Martin and James are really good friends, but I guess technically, Martin is my second.

As Jenna points out, the secondary role does not always indicate a "less than" status in terms of emotional attachment or importance. This person may be loved, highly involved in the primary partners' lives and family, but may not live with them, or may not have as much time or life space with the primaries as the primaries have with each other.

When I asked why some of the other additional partners did not work out, Jenna explained:

> Some people want to be in poly relationships, they believe in it, and care about more than one person, but they can't handle it. Davia was like that—she was with us for months and we tried to work it out. In the end, it was too much drama. She would agree to scheduled times, but then complain she had unexpected needs, or something would come up and she'd ask to trade with me for my time with James, or whatever. I mean, we can be flexible, things aren't written in stone. But we have to keep some kind of order, respect each other's space, you know? It became too negative and emotional and most of the time it seemed she couldn't follow the decisions that we all made together, especially about the time.

In contrast to more in-depth and ongoing polyamorous partnerships like Jenna's, where all partners are on essentially equal ground and well integrated into each other's lives, *seconds* or *thirds* may exist in more casual situations. (I do not use the word *casual* as synonymous with *irresponsible*! Rather, I refer to the formality level of living or meeting arrangements with additional partners.) This type of partner may not seek a more serious relationship. More time may not be expected than all partners can manage for periodic liaisons with one or both primaries.

Flexibility Is Realistic and Necessary

Seconds who have a primary relationship of their own are likely to understand time restrictions. My client, Sharon, handles well being a partner for couples who swing, in part because she herself is in a long-term committed relationship.

Sharon and her boyfriend, Rick, each have outside partners, and they may be the calmest couple I've ever seen with regard to sharing time. In one session Rick did express concern in a very mild manner:

> Sharon and I are pretty clear on what we expect of each other. What got me a little upset was that she spent extra time with this guy, which is unusual for her. I didn't understand why. I can be fine if I know what to expect. Later we talked about it; she explained that it went differently than she thought it would. That doesn't happen usually, but we talked about how there has to be some flexibility because you don't always know how things will go. But overall, we stick to our own rules so we don't have surprises—they can throw me off.

Rick and Sharon have these rules about time that help them feel clear and manage emotions:

- They plan in advance when each of them can have an outside date, often when one is away or very busy with work.
- They tell each other when they will be home. They call if they will be late, and they keep last-minute plan changes to a minimum.
- They plan their *own* time together, and they stick to it.

When multiple partners are involved, variables are common and sticking to plans may not be easy. A bustling family may have trouble getting everyone out the door to school, or consistently being on time to several afterschool activities, while parents have jobs to get to. Multiple partners are all individuals with lives and personalities. As one member of a six-person intimate network complained in my office:

> Invitations to social events always present a challenge! I often don't know which partner I might end up being with and what preferences he might have about attending. It's like a giant family, even though we don't all live together. Have you ever tried to get six people to agree on where to go for dinner and then get them all out their respective doors at the same time?

Compromising and Prioritizing

Just say no. Many people have problems saying no to friends, family, opportunities, and requests. CNM partners have no more time than anyone else. If time is desired with each partner, all must learn to *just say no* to something else. Once priorities are made, partners must also bring their attention to the time made available for sharing. Quality of time spent will otherwise become an issue as well (see Chapter 8).

When clients are overwhelmed with demands and cannot keep up, recommend a time log. Find out what partners are really doing with their time. Each person keeps track on a chart for a week of truthful time expenditures. How much is someone on Facebook? Watching TV or playing games? Working too many hours? After subtracting for sleep, then necessary survival tasks of each day, partners may each have limited time for choices. What is each partner willing to give up? Do partners enjoy group activities together?

While scheduling is a practical matter, emotions impact the process. If jealous or insecure feelings come up, attempts to control schedules of others may be a reaction. Since we cannot control what others feel, choose, or do, attempting to assure our own happiness and security by trying to control the lives of others is not a successful technique. A minister consulted me about some parishioners who were brave enough to ask her advice about an open marriage. The couple was struggling with a situation they had unexpectedly found themselves in and the wife was trying to cope by dictating how each person spent their time. The Reverend shared her experience and professional perspective with me:

> Trying to control people's lives is a dangerous road to walk down. It can lead to emotional manipulation or even abuse. I'm not sure what I think of the open situation this couple is trying to make work, but the controlling behaviors that [parishioner] is resorting to would stunt any relationship, and will breed resentment. What relationship doesn't have time management problems? I see one spouse or the other working longer hours at the office, one picks up a new hobby, another starts spending more time with friends, these days a big issue is time on the computer or playing video games. There needs to be reasonable balance with any activity. But when these things happen, I don't generally hear people say "If you take up photography as a hobby, I am going to schedule when you do it, because I need to limit the amount of time you spend away from me." I don't see people treat hobbies or interests in a time-constraint way. Most couples I've talked with, neither spouse would think it reasonable to say "I'll allow you to play the new video game, but only if you do it for no more than eight hours per month on alternate Wednesdays."
>
> I have to admit that this time with multiple partners issue is no different, though my first tendency—I did see it as different. I had to question my reaction. Time management skills are the same regardless of what or who is demanding the time. I realize it feels different to [wife] when she thinks "My lover is spending time with his other lover" than if the issue was "My lover is spending time in the darkroom." But from a practical perspective, the same tools for managing time still apply. In ministry, I counsel all partners that compassion, respect, clear communication of desires and expectations: these go much further toward creating mutually satisfying relationships than trying to control a partner's time.

Bitsy and Bob, research respondents I interviewed at length (Orion, 2008) have been married for 32 years in consensual nonmonogamy. They both work. They have three adult children. Bob has had two female lovers for most of those years. Bitsy and Jason, Bob's best friend, have always been close and shared periodic liaisons throughout the years and they often talk by phone. When asked about time management arrangements, Bitsy shared the following:

> I used to think I wanted a live-in poly arrangement with somebody (laughs) but over the years I realized I don't. I know Bob's women, they're both really extraordinary, actually. Neither one lives here in (big city USA) so it's not like we had to figure things out on a daily basis. But when our kids were little, I needed Bob around! [One of Bob's girlfriends] would come into town and he'd be like—I have to go NOW! No warning! A couple times I got upset. We had a few fights about it. For me, it's easier because Jason lives here [in same city]. He's busy and we don't get together that often, but we

have access to each other all the time. Still, me and Bob had to talk! Family time had to come first, even if it meant that he missed an opportunity to see one of them.

Bitsy brings up an issue in CNM that may come up with secondary partners: Even when time scheduling is working well for all partners involved, a secondary partner may have unexpected needs, impacting routines. The additional partner could get sick and need care, or hopes the primary partner will attend a special event that is scheduled during a different partner's allotted time. Bob admits:

> I was always the offender! My wife is so awesome; she accepts that I have two lovers, really good friends to both of us. They both live out of town. I met each one—Jewel and Diane—at different times, years ago now. When either one can get here, the priority is going to be me having time with her. Sometimes we don't know much in advance. Jewel is married but her partner was out of town once when she had an accident. I flew there. Dan [Jewel's husband] was really glad I could, she was in the hospital and he was across the world! We were all worried. The timing was terrible because I had plans with Bitsy, but she didn't blink over that one. She was just as worried as I was and, let's face it, she has a good heart! We did make a point of rescheduling our weekend though. We had to wait three weeks to get the time! But I mean, if you care about someone, you have to show up in an emergency. Some of the other times Bits has put the kybosh on my running off at the last minute. Even if we didn't have plans. The kids were a lot—we both had to be there and I get it. I've babysat so she could see Jason, I will say that. Sometimes I felt it wasn't entirely fair. We went around a few times about some of the occasions but you know what? It's my marriage and my family. In the long run, the times she's uncomfortable with me having a date, I have to respect that.

Kenny and Krista are a good example of a primary couple struggling for quality time. They see mutual friends on occasions when all the busy people involved are able to make time to be together. Krista experienced feelings of jealousy having to do with how Kenny was managing his time and how little time they were spending together on their own relationship.

In a therapy session Krista relates:

> Kenny has worked really hard with our son. I'm still struggling with our couple issues; frankly, he didn't keep up with our weekly dates. And when we do see our friends for sex, I don't get his attention at all. Its like I'm not even there with him. That's something else to work on, but I have to give him credit for changing his life around to be with our son every day, do more with him all the time. Our family time is a lot improved. It was part of what upset me and it's made a lot of difference to me and the baby. Whatever our lifestyle is going to be, we both do feel that family comes first and Kenny just

hadn't watched how much he was working and being out with friends when it was important times for [our son]. Now he's home at bedtimes a lot more and spends family time with me and the baby.

Whatever happens with Kenny and Krista's sex life, they are clear that being parents is their first responsibility and is fundamental to the rest of their relationship. Parenting takes a lot of time. No matter how many caregivers are involved in a CNM situation, keeping the sexual issues separate from responsibilities to children, including all the time allotment required, is imperative.

Family first is an important principle in successful quality CNM time management. Jill and Jack made this a basis for Jack's outside relationships. They've had a *don't ask, don't tell* agreement for over twenty years. Jill long ago lost her interest in having sex, but didn't want Jack to leave. Jack didn't want to cheat or leave but was going crazy. They created an open situation, but Jill didn't want to know details of Jack's other relationships. She explains,

> One of my rules is that Jack's plans can't interfere with family time. For the most part Jack has always respected this. A few times in the beginning we had to learn better communication because he made a couple of plans that screwed us up, but I honestly think he didn't mean to. I didn't want to be talking with him about what he was doing so we had to figure out how to make sure he planned with our son and family stuff first. But how do we do that if I don't want to talk about his plans? So we made the family calendar. It worked!

Assessments

Understand the General CNM Arrangement

Do partners have specified time allotments and agreements in place? If not, why not? Did none of them think of it, or realize it could be necessary? Do they all want to just be spontaneous? (Ha!) Does each think the others have the same expectations and understandings which, however, have not been clearly examined nor discussed? If arrangements are in place, have each partner explain their personal understanding of these. If the plans are not working, what does each partner think is going wrong?

Gain the Necessary Information

Clinicians who do not already know the answers to these contextual questions, which impact how time decisions are made, should understand the following needs to be determined:

- How many partners are involved? How many, and in what roles, are complaining about time or other issues that may be affected by time?

- How long has each partner been involved in any, and in this particular, CNM relationship? (How experienced are any of them in dealing with CNM issues?)
- How casual or formal are the partners' living and meeting arrangements?
- Are there children involved? How well do caregivers manage the children and *their* time requirements?
- Does each person's time include self-care? An overstressed or unwell individual is already at a disadvantage and may be more needy, seeking (and possibly ought to get) more time and care from others.
- Did problems arise when a new person entered the picture, adding to time-sharing requirements?
- When partners do spend time together, assess quality. What are they doing? Do they pay attention to each other? Are they overusing electronics? Is either partner really focusing on something or someone else, rather than the person with whom time is being shared? Are they sharing activities they both or all enjoy?
- What has already been tried in attempts to resolve or adjust time issues?

The Role of Clinicians

When partners talk things out with a therapist—a nonjudgmental moderator—this can do a lot toward sorting and resolving problems. Each partner may hear new ideas and information and get support for personal feelings. It is unlikely that time and space issues come without attached feelings and relational problems, but getting control of time use and how attention is focused (see Chapter 8) can go a long way toward clarifying and clearing up the less practical problems.

Facilitating clear communication when plans are being discussed is paramount. Provide nonjudgmental support for feelings. Teach "I" language, active listening, and compassionate listening. Make sure each partner is being clear and complete when asking for what they want. Tyrell, Chena, and Carol, clients, illustrate some simple communication problems. Tyrell says to Chena and Carol, who vie for his time:

> Often at least one of you will make assumptions about me without asking, you just assume based on what you think I was just doing. Or you don't say clearly what you expect, and then you're mad and hurt if the expectations aren't met. You can't just say "The new Batman movie is coming out next Friday." From that, I think you're just having a conversation. Next thing I know one of you is mad because I didn't ask you to the movie. You have to say "The new Batman movie is coming out next Friday, and it's really important to me to that you take me to the opening." . . . Like, you have to finish the sentence, say what you really mean.

Unstated expectations can become toxic to any relationship. Counsel CNM clients to state thoughts and feelings completely, express needs clearly and directly, without implied and unspoken assumptions. Partners cannot read each other's minds. The old idea that "If s/he really loved me, s/he would know my needs, and know without me saying that I want thus-and-such" is a sure way that any given partner won't get what they want; unexpressed emotions and unmet needs will burst out later, causing drama.

Summary of Useful Techniques

- Present to, or create with clients, practical ideas, such as a family calendar.
- Ask partners what problems and ideas they have with regard to creating, organizing, and following schedules.
- Help create realistic time arrangements with each partner, with family and children as first priorities.
- Help individuals who have poor time management skills and poor self-care to gain these skills. These are basic to the health and functioning of all relationships in the group.
- Help individuals within the group manage feelings, communicate, self-soothe, and learn calming skills.
- Help individuals be clear on their own absolute needs and where they can be flexible. If they want or need this kind of relationship, all partners likely have to compromise some.
- If problems arose when a new partner entered the picture, help locate or create ways to make room for this person. Feelings and issues may have arisen that none have talked about clearly, or if discussed, were not resolved. Facilitate honest discussion. Maybe the new person just won't work out, but all partners can determine better if they are a match after sharing feelings, sorting out practicalities from other issues, and trying any interventions.
- Teach or provide resources for learning mindfulness (Chapter 8).

Reference

Orion, R. (2008). *From traditional to open marriage.* Case study report. San Francisco: Saybrook Graduate School & Research Center.

Case Excerpt: Kim and Ranger

Kim and Ranger were clients. They attended sessions sporadically over the course of a year, some as a couple and some as individuals. Each had learned from previous relationships that traditional monogamy is not ideal for them. Personal mental health issues, unclear rules, and not following agreements challenge an initially successful expanded monogamy marriage. Assessments and discussion of interventions are intertwined throughout the report of their story.

Kim is a 42-year-old physician; Ranger is an attorney, age 43. Kim and Ranger met in high school, dating off and on for a decade. Later going in different directions, they each married someone else for several years only to get back in touch and marry each other. They have two children, one in elementary and the other in middle school. Though both have demanding jobs, Ranger works some hours at home while providing child care and Kim gets frequent vacations and long weekends to spend with family.

Ranger has a steady relationship with Allyssa, the wife of a couple who are friends of Kim and Ranger. Allyssa's husband is less enthusiastic about CNM, in part, because he has no outside relationship of his own, but he does condone Allyssa's relationship with Ranger. He and Allyssa have a fairly stringent allowance for her time with Ranger, and while they are open about CNM, Allyssa's marriage is strained.

Ranger doesn't get to see Allyssa as often as either he or she would like, and Kim has several boyfriends she can call at any given time. Resentment has been building between Kim and Ranger, which he talks about:

> It's not that she has more beaus. I get that she has problems with longer-term partners. She's still a hot woman and can attract guys she thinks are exciting. I don't need a lot of lovers, Allyssa and I grew out of friendship and we mean something to each other. And she's a friend of the family. But not every guy of Kim's wants to hear about, let alone meet, the husband of his fun-time lover! Allyssa and I have a real relationship and I appreciate that [her husband] is allowing it, I really do. He's kind of a conservative guy, but Allyssa was honest with him when our interest sparked. He did cheat on her in the past and sees how feelings for someone else can arise. He wanted to try being honest and making rules about it. They've worked at it for a couple

years now. Allyssa's marriage is important to her and takes priority over us. I get that. I respect that. I feel the same way!

My problem is that Kim doesn't stick to our agreements. She's constantly asking for more or special time with one guy or another. She's frequently not come home when we'd agreed. She'll call, it's not that I don't know where she is. It's that I end up having to deal with the kids unexpectedly or for longer than planned. I've sometimes given up time with Allyssa because of it or for our family. Kim will apologize but then it happens again. Kim's been with a lot of guys since the day we met. We've always thought the same about monogamy—it's not for us. But now we have a family and a commitment to each other. There have to be limits.

Kim doesn't deny any of what Ranger says. She also shares more about her problems with parenting:

He's great with the kids. My daughter has come right out and told me they'd rather be with daddy. They tell him mommy's "mean." I don't hit them or anything! I'm distracted. I get annoyed. I don't have patience. I have this saying: I'm good with patients but not with patience. I'm a great doctor but I think I must be a terrible mother [cries]. I really feel bad when I let Ranger down, and I know I'm missing out on the kids' lives. But when I'm with someone else, having a great time, and the sex is exciting, I feel so much better. That relationship is so important at the time. It always seems reasonable to me to stay longer, or promise another date or trip before I've talked with Ranger. The kids don't seem to want to be with me anyway. It always makes sense at the time, until I'm back and Ranger and I have another fight about it. I know he's right.

Ranger grew up with a single mother who was clinically schizophrenic. They were frequently homeless, living for periods of time with one of his mother's friends or another, a scattered relative, a short-term rental. Even as a child, Ranger knew that his mother was sick. He did have some feeling that he ought to be able to help her; he tried to take care of her in any way he could think of. She was, however, for the most part just not there emotionally or as a mother.

Ranger managed to stay in school. When there was no reason to be at whatever place was currently home, he spent hours in the library literally "holed up reading." As a teen and an adult, he came to understand his mother's illness. Eventually a grandparent took him in. He graduated high school and went on to college. He and Kim dated and stayed in touch off and on; however, he went to college far from her and met his first wife.

While Ranger deals with anxiety and still feels some effects of early neglect, he managed to develop into a relatively stable man and father. It does not help him, however, to feel neglected by his wife, or to see her put her children as second priority. He married a neglectful woman who can't seem to stay in one place emotionally and runs from place to place for various liaisons.

Ranger states, "Kim and I always had a special connection. She was a mess, but we were connected when together like in no other relationships either of us have had. Eventually she got it together and it takes a lot to get through medical school."

Kim was also neglected in some ways as well as traumatized because her father was emotionally and physically abusive to Kim's mother. When Kim was 12 years old, her mother took Kim and her brother and ran. Like Ranger, Kim went from one living situation to another as her family tried to stay one step ahead of the abusive father. In her teen years, Kim was drinking and using drugs. As her mother had to keep them all on the run, Kim dropped out of high school and slept with various boys.

Eventually Kim's mother got legal help and a decent job in a fairly large town where they were able to settle down. Kim waitressed and did various other low-paying jobs. She and Ranger had continued to see each other even though Kim was sleeping with other boys and doing drugs. He repeatedly encouraged her to get help and back to school. When he went away to a distant college, they still saw each other summers, and Kim experienced other more long-term relationships.

During one visit with Ranger, Kim finally decided to take his advice. Even though he returned to college in another state, she stopped drinking and doing drugs on her own and went back to school. She continued on to become a physician, also marrying for the first time, another medical student.

A job brought her back into the vicinity of Ranger. A casual communication to catch up as old friends revealed they still had the same special connection. Neither was happy in their respective marriage. They got back together, both professionals and wanting a family.

Ranger has done much to understand and heal from his childhood and teen years with a mentally ill parent. His temperament is stable and he is able to develop long-term intimacy, as well as be a parent who is reliable and calm. Kim has stayed clean from drugs and, despite constantly moving as a child which negatively affected her schooling, she has become a respected physician. Emotionally, however, she still displays behaviors resulting from fear, instability, and addiction. This is reflected in her behaviors at home and her choices of secondary partners.

The overriding behavioral problem in this CNM marriage is that Kim is unable to follow whatever agreements she and Ranger make with regard to scheduling and child care. Her unresolved past of running from an abusive father is reflected in her "mean" parenting style and in making her children less important than whatever current excitement she feels with a secondary partner. Constant running as young girl from one situation to the next for safety gave her hope in each new port with her mother. Soon the situation would be unsafe again and the two would run to the next possible safe place. This experience may be reflected in her current-day behavior of running from secondary partner to secondary partner, as each one seems to hold new promise and excitement.

Through biweekly sessions, Kim came to see that her past was hurting her and her children, as well as sabotaging her marriage. The problem was not that she had other sex partners, but that she did not keep to agreements and schedules about those partners: not coming home as promised, leaving Ranger in the lurch, not showing up for family plans, making arrangements longer than she and Ranger had agreed without talking with him. She apologizes repeatedly but does not change her behavior. In addition, she at times ruins Ranger's time with Allyssa by drinking, displaying jealousy, and being insulting.

Ranger realizes through therapy that he is extra-sensitive to the neglect he feels from Kim, who, after several years of marriage, seemed to care more about other men. They always had open arrangements, but Ranger said that Kim used to show more genuine excitement and love for him. They still felt their special connection, but she did things for him in the past that had dwindled in the last year or so. Her unreliable and irresponsible behaviors have escalated at the same time.

Discussion

Kim's mental health issues and resulting behaviors are a major issue in this relationship. Ranger's past makes it especially difficult for him to deal with Kim's choices and unreliability. Their time arrangements are unclear and they have unequal time with other partners. The relationship may be helped if both of them work enough on their personal mental and emotional health to be able to create and carry out agreements.

They agreed to create practical, realistic plans and schedules that put children first and don't overburden one parent over the other, as possible. If change is desired or must be made, discuss this together first. Communication skills could be improved, and used during regular discussions about family care and how their CNM plans are working.

Kim claimed she'd limit drinking when with any of her partners and when Allyssa is visiting, so she can control her behavior and stick to commitments. Ideally, Kim needs to learn mindfulness, self-soothing, self-discipline techniques, and positive parenting skills.

Mindfulness was also discussed with Ranger to help him with generalized anxiety and residual feelings from his past. He's learning skills for speaking up effectively about his own needs in the family and relationship. He tends to let slide too much before saying anything to Kim, at which point he's already upset while she thinks everything has been fine.

To strengthen their marriage, Kim and Ranger agreed to plan fun dates with each other keeping outside partners uninvolved, even via texting or calls. If either has to cancel their married couples date, success requires rescheduling any time meant to be spent together as a primary couple. If improvements in their relationship become apparent, Ranger and Kim may benefit from a series of sensate focus exercises to improve intimacy and support their personal bond.

Kim and Ranger tried to implement these ideas and plans for a few months. While Kim began to see how her own issues were causing problems, she had limited success in following through on agreements. She drank less often but overall did not make a big change in substance abuse when she was not working. While she had limited success changing her behaviors with men during the few months she attended therapy sessions, she did change how she parented and made inroads in repairing and improving relationships with her children. She started employing some positive parenting routines, calming herself before spending time with her kids, and staying focused on them while together. She learned she can have fun with them, a discovery that brought her to tears when she relayed it.

Ranger grew stronger in his stands about his and Kim's commitments and his needs in their relationship. This was positive, but his patience more quickly waned with Kim's repeated scheduling mess-ups and emotional betrayals. She would agree in sessions to new plans but still not follow through. Ranger was tired of not having time with Allyssa when it was Kim's unreliability (and time with her secondary partners) that caused problems.

After a few months of sessions and trying new things that Kim couldn't do with enough consistency, Ranger wanted to try living separately. They own two places due to travel and jobs in various locations plus a vacation condo, each of which is familiar to the children.

Ranger felt that Kim would be forced to keep to her time agreements, including childcaring time, if they lived in separate places, because he would not "just be around" all the time. In addition, he felt that if Kim wanted time with him, then they'd have to arrange it like a date, and she might treat him differently when they were together. He would have privacy during the limited hours he could spend with Allyssa. He felt that he and Kim would argue less. And most importantly he felt the children would have more calm and focused attention when with their mother.

Ranger saw the idea of having separate abodes as standing up for himself, and as a way to keep their relationship under less pressure while Kim did more personal healing work. Kim was extremely threatened by the idea of a separation, even though she agreed that it could help. Kim admitted that she needs more personal work, including with alcohol abuse, and that so far she had gained a lot through therapy. Kim and Ranger remain married and living out of two different places. They continue to struggle with supporting each other's additional partnerships, but some problems have been eliminated because they are not living together.

8 Attention and Mindfulness in Consensual Nonmonogamy

What a powerful force is attention! The ability to focus, or lack thereof, is an issue affecting health, relationships, success, and daily living. In consensual nonmonogamy (CNM), attention to multiple personal relationships is especially demanding.

No one has endless energy and attention to give. In connection with others, each individual's mental and physical health is important—and at possible risk. As a sex and relationship therapist I have heard countless problems and complaints from CNM clients caused by attention issues. In CNM there are more relationships involved, thus more potential difficulties with attention and connection between and among partners.

Many important words and concepts are bandied about in relationships, often unexamined by users. According to the Merriam-Webster dictionary, "attention" has several definitions, three of which apply to human relations. I have modified the given examples of each to personalize relationship situations:

1   The act or state of applying the mind to something: *You need to pay attention to what she says.* A condition of readiness for such attention—a selective narrowing or focusing of consciousness and receptivity: *Darling, do I have your attention?*
2   Observation, notice: *Dear, do you see what's going on?* Consideration with a view to action: *Honey, this is a problem requiring prompt attention.*
3   An act of civility or courtesy, especially in courtship: *She welcomed his attentions.* Sympathetic consideration of the needs and wants of others.
4   Attentiveness: *She lavished attention on her partner.*

These action definitions are particularly useful in parenting and other intimate relationships. It is desirable for partners to *apply their minds*, to *focus* their *consciousness and receptivity*, to observe and respond, and to have *sympathetic consideration of the needs and wants of others*. I would be surprised at a partner who would not enjoy some *lavish attention!*

The behaviors carrying out these attentions may need clarification in any set of CNM relationships. As with *trust* and *honesty*, several partners may use the same terms but act on them differently from one another's expectations.

These definitions of attention, however, leave out the self as a receiver. Attention is also something to focus inwardly; this attention to self has come to be called *mindfulness*. Research now abounds on mindfulness (Baer, 2003; Deninger, Lazar, & Vego, 2016; Hoge et al., 2017; Kabat-Zinn, 1979/2013; Kemeny, 2016; Siegel, 2007). Mindfulness can be described as *being in the present moment with one's mind and attention*. Many therapists teach Mindfulness-Based Stress Reduction (MBSR)©. This was founded by Dr. Jon Kabat-Zinn in 1979 and is the subject of his book, *Full Catastrophe Living* (1979/2013). MBSR is primarily about the systematic training and refinement of attention and awareness, compassion, and wisdom. So much has been discovered about the improvement of mental and physical health when people practice mindfulness regularly (Baer, 2003; Deninger et al., 2016; Hoge et al., 2017; Kabat-Zinn, 1979/2013; Kemeny, 2016; Siegel, 2007), even a few minutes a day, or in small ways woven into their daily activities, that it seems almost malpractice not to discuss this with clients, regardless of the presenting problem. It is similar to a dentist promoting tooth brushing, or a physician stating the necessity of exercise and proper nutrition.

Mindfulness is free, does not have to be time-consuming, has no negative side effects, and virtually anyone can practice it. Studies with children and teens (Greenberg & Alexis, 2011) learning mindfulness in schools have shown remarkable results. Mindfulness, which helps understanding of one's attention and focus, can change individual health, relationships, and family dynamics for the better.

The Merriam-Webster dictionary defines *mindfulness* as:

1   The quality or state of being *aware*.
2   The practice of maintaining a nonjudgmental state of heightened or complete awareness of one's thoughts, emotions, or experiences on a moment-to-moment basis.

A lack of mindfulness is another way of saying *attention problems*. Resolving these issues begins with *awareness of one's thoughts, emotions, or experiences on a moment-to-moment basis*. First, we must recognize what's going on within us. Sometimes that is enough to calm or change interference with attentiveness. Without awareness of what our inner reality is, we cannot make wise choices. Knowledge opens the way for intelligent changes.

Feelings are multiplied in CNM relationships. A common saying in therapy is *You can't heal what you don't feel*. Awareness of feelings underlies appropriate expression and behaviors. Feelings are often buried beneath coping mechanisms now outdated and hiding trauma. Mindfulness helps individuals become aware of their underlying feelings, needs, and processes; mindfulness supports calm, thoughtful response as opposed to unexamined, triggered reactions.

Partners in CNM relationships are encouraged to learn mindfulness because:

• It helps those with attention problems gain control over focus, memory, completion of tasks, and attention span.

- It helps clarity of feelings in complex situations.
- It helps individuals to remain calm when discussing emotionally charged issues and agreements.
- It helps tolerance and positivity with regard to compromise and sharing.
- It helps maintain physical and mental health in busy and demanding lives.
- It helps healing from past traumas which impact all relationships and parenting.
- It helps improve sexual and intimate connection.
- It helps change brain chemistry and improve the immune system.
- It helps attention and mindfulness: Attention to the other emerging from attention to the self.

Evaluation of Attention Issues

Being in the moment and paying attention to self and others are skills that do not come naturally to many. It may be necessary to examine what clients are doing with the attention they do receive, as well as how they are reaching out for connection. Evaluate the following:

- unexamined expectations of what *attention* means to any client;
- problems each individual may have with the type and amount of attention they had in their family of origin;
- how past experiences translate into their relationships and CNM arrangements (*I never get enough time with . . .*);
- traumas and their impact on the individual and all relationships in the CNM partnership;
- ongoing health issues—a person may need more attention or be unable to give certain types or amounts of attention;
- how much, and the quality of, attention that is ongoing—an accounting by all partners of when and why attention is (or is not) shared, given, or received.

Problems with Attention in CNM

Clients who already lack self-awareness or have difficulties with focus and attention are challenged in CNM. Let's examine each of these specific issues:

- misdirected attention seeking;
- sexual and intimacy issues;
- overwhelmed by multiple relationship attention demands;
- brain problems with focus and attention.

Misdirected Attention Seeking

There is a difference between seeking attention in unhealthy ways and being *attentive together with another human being*. Attention seekers do need attention! But their personal growth does not benefit from attention received, unless they understand why they need attention, and examine the effectiveness of methods employed to achieve what they seek.

Time and attention are shared in CNM. Partners have to care for themselves at times, rather than being able to be with another. Underlying reasons for wanting attention may be due to childhood experiences or other issues that need to come into awareness. Such reasons, unexamined, can cause problems with time-sharing in CNM, as well as resulting in lack of satisfaction with attention that is received. A partner may need to learn skills of evaluating personal emotions and behaviors when seeking the attention of others. Self-soothing skills may be necessary—attention to one's own mind and heart.

Carrie is a client who struggles with alcoholism. She grew up with an emotionally abusive father and a mother and grandmother whom Carrie could never please, no matter what she did. She rarely received positive attention that supported her true self or her achievements. She was attracted to consensual non-monogamy, she learned, in part because there are more partners to give her different kinds of attention. This is a healing experience for her, because neither of her partners is emotionally abusive. They are, however, busy, and neither one is constantly around to be with Carrie. She seemed never satisfied with the time spent with either partner, nor with what they would all do when together. Even if she had a good time or one of them did something to show affection and appreciation, her happiness was short-lived and she would then complain and blame. This is not a pattern enjoyed by her partners. Her upsets often led to her picking up several drinks—her habitual way of self-soothing—which predictably worsened her behavior.

Carrie came into therapy feeling as though neither of her partners cared enough about her. "I have two guys and I'm still lonely! I'm not sure either one of them appreciates me. I also want to have another baby, but neither Carl nor Randy thinks it's a good idea. You'd think that at least one of them would be there for me!"

I point out to Carrie that she is struggling with alcohol abuse, an abuse not acceptable when planning a pregnancy, nor in parenting a child. Carrie has been regularly attending an outpatient addiction program and doing well, but she started this only a couple of months prior to seeing me—not long enough to trust her changes in behavior nor assure consistent sobriety.

Through journaling and therapy Carrie became clear for the first time on why she felt her partners didn't care enough about her.

> We had this assignment [in addiction program] to write about our family of origin and how we felt growing up. I realized that I want to care for people and I'm longing for a baby because a baby loves you back. When my

daughter was a baby she and I felt connected, I knew my caring about her worked. I never had that feeling when I was growing up! No matter what I did I never felt it worked—that I'd get attention and love.

I explained to Carrie that this childhood experience of not getting needed love and attention is still affecting her in another way: She doesn't recognize, nor know how to let in, genuine attention from her partners. Further, she had described situations in daily life with Carl and Randy wherein she would "set up" a failure, because this is what her brain knows how to do with regard to attention—make sure that whatever she does "won't work."

Childhood experiences not understood predict future perspectives and behaviors. Carrie was able to learn when her negative past experiences are coloring her present positive ones. Through cognitive behavioral therapy, including 10-minute mindfulness exercises several days a week, Carrie expressed a greater ability to slow down her thinking and behaviors, giving her time to assess and choose new responses.

Instead of reacting, which is what I was doing, I can take a breath and evaluate if Carl or Randy is trying to show me love, or get *my* attention—I hadn't realized that I was actually shutting *them* out half the time. I'm not perfect but they see now when I choose a new response instead of just going off the rails like I used to. I was missing so much of what I needed, because I wasn't aware of my own thoughts and feelings, or how I was keeping love away so I could be mad and lonely like I was used to [while growing up]. I've had to learn to deal with bad feelings and thoughts without picking up a drink. [My partners] are being supportive and I see that now!

Sexual and Intimacy Issues

CNM partners share multiple and varied sexual experiences. Being mindful in each relationship helps maintain the special connection each person has with each partner. People are not interchangeable; one partner does not replace another. But an underlying reason why some feel threatened in multiple partnerships is that they begin to question their own worth, their own intimate and special connection with a particular partner. Mindfulness is a powerful tool to help each partner feel personal value, to self-soothe, to express emotions more clearly and calmly, and to more strongly experience the unique connection with each partner.

Intimate and unique connection is not all about sex. Sex is, however, both a powerful and fragile aspect of some intimate partnerships. Sex is one difference between CNM and just having more friends or roommates. In CNM, it is easy to compare the quality of intimate and sexual time of each set of partners. (*Do you have better sex with partner A than with me?*) It is desirable for each partnership to maintain a unique sexual connection.

Mechanical or routine sex is never reported in my office as desirable and often leads to *no* sex, a situation that can stress and dissolve relationships. Conversely, "good" sex can keep some relationships together. But what is "good" sex? The few studies (Kleinplatz et al., 2009) I know of that explore positives as opposed to pathology reveal that *optimal sex* is *connected sex,* and is about more than genital pleasure. Data from respondents who were interviewed about their self-described optimal sex experiences revealed eight top components, none of which had to do specifically with orgasm or intercourse: being present, connection, deep sexual and erotic intimacy, extraordinary communication, interpersonal risk-taking and exploration, authenticity, vulnerability, and transcendence.

Respondents shared their personal experiences with phrases such as:

- We felt like one, yet still two beings.
- Time went away.
- We were in our own world and completely connected.
- I felt totally safe and WITH my partner.
- I could be myself no matter what.
- We were together with each other, and with God.

These statements describe mindful sex as opposed to distracted, disconnected, or routine sex.

Optimal sex, or even just "good" sex, often requires learned skills, high self-esteem, core comfort with one's own sexuality and with sexual expression, well-developed communication skills, and a brain that allows flow activities. Certified sex therapists are trained to provide in-depth help with these aspects.

Overwhelmed by Multiple Relationship Attention Demands

Help clients learn to prepare the mind or, as the Merriam-Webster dictionary puts it, gain "a condition of readiness for such attention." Who hasn't heard a client talk about being bombarded the minute of getting home after a long work-day? Are the partner and kids just waiting for mom or dad to walk into the house? Comedian Chris Rock (1999) performs a standup routine about relationships. "Let me get situated, get my other foot in the door . . . let me get something to drink . . . let me [use the bathroom] . . ." he declares, before he is assailed with nonstop talking and demands the minute he gets home.

I encourage parents and partners to do what I call *shifting the focus*: take a few moments on their way home from a busy day to deliberately shift their brain focus. Take a deep breath and use self-talk: *I'm coming home now. There will be a wife (partners, children) who have had days of their own and may have been waiting for me. I need to connect when I get in the door, or as soon thereafter as possible, even for a few moments.* Those at home can also prepare by realizing that daddy (mommy, partner) is soon to arrive, and seek to offer greeting with a little calm and connection; give the homecomer a chance to *get situated*, get both feet in the door—to fully arrive, and to take care of any urgent personal needs.

Recommend that clients share partner or family meals. Supper is traditionally a time for connection at the end of a day, a time for sharing personal and physical nourishment; a time to *just eat*, to *just be with* one another, to catch up on and assess the day. If suppertime isn't possible, create a different regular time to share food or tea and talk. When partners and family members know that such a time is regularly planned, each can count on time for shared, focused attention. When we know that our needs will be met, feelings of security are supported and it is easier to wait for needs to be fulfilled.

Creating space and time for focused attention, and preparing the mind's focus, are interventions that help integrate mindfulness into daily life. These tools can help anyone, but specific to CNM apply to:

- a partner coming back to the primary one, after seeing a second partner;
- a partner coming home to two or more other partners;
- a partner leaving home, preparing to meet with another;
- any poly partner returning to partner(s) and children.

Consciously preparing to change situations or partners, or to return to family, takes only mindful moments. Then a tone is set. Children, adults, and animals do get it when genuine attention is paid. Before the concept of mindfulness existed, my dear mother always said about my toddlers, "Give them 5 minutes of real attention, then they're good for 20 minutes on their own." Twenty minutes may not be the result with all toddlers! But translated to adults paying attention to each other, those who learn ways to share connection in moments, minutes, and mini tasks throughout their days report to me more overall happiness and intimacy. They also complain less about differences and other partners' annoying habits.

Brain Problems with Focus and Attention

Anxiety, depression, PTSD, and physical ailments and impairments can negatively impact ability to pay attention and connect with others. Treating these issues in CNM utilizes general therapy skills. Multiple committed partners, however, need to be aware of all other partners' symptoms, know how to manage resulting stress, and learn how to support one another in healing and change. With CNM clients, clinicians are potentially treating multiple partners, even if only one comes to the office.

The "Gifted Brain" in Consensual Nonmonogamy

In my experience, one of the most prevalent problems of attention in relationships is the set of symptoms and issues commonly diagnosed in the United States as attention deficit disorder (ADD). This cluster of symptoms can result from trauma and may join other patterns such as obsessive-compulsive disorder (OCD) and post-traumatic stress disorder (PTSD). Relating to others is particularly difficult when any of these diagnoses are present; combining several adults who relate intimately and may each have some degree of any of these disorders presents a challenge.

ADD is the most prevalent of this class of problems in my experience, because in addition to resulting from trauma, the symptoms called ADD are seen as inherent in many children, teens, and adults. Because ADD in CNM relationships causes trouble for multiple partners I am discussing it here. I also introduce my alternate perspective on, and my term for, the ADD brain.

I am in the psychological camp that espouses a more positive view of ADD or ADHD (attention deficit hyperactivity disorder). The patterns of behavior and issues with brain function that people complain about are real—forgetfulness, hyper focus, disorganization, short attention span, easily distracted, unfinished tasks, difficulty with emotions and personal connection—among others. The individual may be messy and live in clutter or, alternatively, have obsessive-compulsive tendencies. I have found frequently, however, that such children, teens, and adults tend to be excessively smart or artistically talented. They may also vary in learning styles from the larger population. This group of cognitive, emotional, and behavioral difficulties may be common to any type of relationship throughout the lifespan, but differ in CNM because there are more arrangements and partners needing focused attention, more issues needing to be kept straight, more details and plans that need following, in order for CNM to work.

Medical model diagnostics vilify the ADD type of person based on the difficulties listed, labeling these difficulties as a *deficiency disorder*. I believe these persons have what I call "gifted brains" and can learn skills to manage or transform the "deficiencies." We ought to value the intelligence and talents (which seem to make their brains a bit lopsided when it comes to some order and memory skills), while teaching such persons the needed organizational, focus, calming, and memory skills.

Everyone isn't good at the same things. A gifted surgeon may not be good at paying attention to her husband. A genius with computers may be terrible at housekeeping. An organized, outgoing event planner may be poor at intimacy skills. Someone who can paint beautiful portraits may be forgetful and disheveled. Some CNM partners take the necessary challenges in their stride, and others struggle with several aspects that require the exact skills sometimes lacking in gifted brain persons.

As a former art history student, I know that Michelangelo is reported to have worked for days and nights on end, forgetting to eat, drink, or wash. Friends would bring him food and there's a story that his shoes (made of animal skin) literally adhered to his flesh when he was working on his David statue because he refused to leave his work even to cleanse himself. These days, he would likely have been diagnosed with ADD, OCD, and possibly more, and medicated.

What kind of person would lie on his back, for months on end, over a hundred feet in the air, to paint a ceiling? Or spend his life obsessed with understanding light, as Einstein did—a man who changed the world's knowledge of the universe and science. Einstein was berated as a child and college student due to his lack of attention and refusal to follow rules. He was repeatedly told that academically, he'd amount to nothing.

What does this have to do with consensual nonmonogamy? Unless already aware and skilled at managing a gifted brain, these individuals are likely forgetful and may not "get" a lot of things that others know. Behaviors that can bother partners and impact childcare, such as not remembering tasks needing to be done routinely, the favorite things of a partner or child, or health needs of loved ones. These persons may also be poor at self-care, affecting how well they relate to and care for others. A lot of processing, communication, and managing emotions of self and others are required in CNM. Gifted brain people especially have difficulty learning and adopting new routines. They often cannot manage to take in and process much at a time in conversations, especially emotional ones. These partners are likely disorganized in general and may have a tendency to collect stuff—a nice way of saying they hoard—affecting the environment of all partners and children involved.

How time is divided and shared is a major component of CNM relationships. When partners have time together, it needs to be quality time with minds in the moment, focused on one another's mutual experiences. This is difficult for gifted brain persons. One of my CNM clients, Victoria, complained that when she finally had time with her husband, he paid her no focused attention. "I may as well not even be in the room," she said. In addition, when they had shared sex nights with friends, he did pay attention to someone else. "He *can* focus his attention—why not with me?" Victoria was understandably hurt. She—and her husband—needed to understand that his attention is not always under his control and can be hijacked by a variety of stimuli.

If it's not some *one* else taking that gifted brain person's attention, it may be some *thing* else. The effect of electronics on health and brain function has become a topic in many professions. Technological devices now impact the attention span and focus of spouses, partners, parents, and children with possible deleterious effects on brains, individuals, and relationships.

Carla, Carl, and Ronny are partners who are all affected by Ronny's constant time at the computer. Carla explains:

> When it's work, we understand. But half the time we look and he's playing games, or on Facebook or something else meaningless for hours! We feel like he'd rather sit at his computer than pay attention to either one of us. When we get him to be with us, it's like his brain isn't there with us anymore. Like he's still thinking about the computer.

Assessing Brain Issues

The following may guide the therapist in discerning if and how gifted brain problems are impacting a CNM relationship:

- Who in the set of partners has gifted brain and resulting behaviors?
- How is each person impacted by the partner with these symptoms?

- How does the gifted brain person feel about, and view, her or his part in the reported relationship complaints? Is this person aware of how the brain works and the resulting behavioral symptoms?
- What has each partner, including the gifted brain person, already done or tried, to address the issue?
- Is the person on medications, and if so, does that help or hinder? Are there side effects?

Helping Brain Issues

Usually others are doing a lot of reminding for such persons, covering for them when they forget important things, trying to get them to adopt healthy habits and to learn to manage their own lives. One frustrated client declared to me:

> I don't know how he does it! Three times now he's gone to a doctor on the wrong day—and talked them into seeing him! He's got charm! But it's like, why should he take my advice and use calendars, and reminders—he loves his phone enough! He's learned how to talk his way around mistakes, and he is genuinely sorry when things impact me at home. But he doesn't change, even though he's not stupid! I mean, the man is a genius—two advanced degrees—but he can't remember how to load the dishwasher, or what kind of flowers I like. (I hate the smell of lilies!) I find his half-chewed cigars all over the house, even right next to the trash can. These seem like small things, it's just that there's such a list of many small things every day. And when he does do something to help, there's always a problem. He doesn't finish the job, or he leaves the mess. Or he puts stuff back in the wrong place, oh, it's endless! When I try to talk about anything, he can't pay attention long enough, and gets mad saying his "head will explode" if he has to hear one more detail. He wants to meet some prospective sex date partners like we used to, but how can we do that if he can't even have a conversation about rules?

Sorting out the responsibility of the gifted brain person's need to learn, vs. what others can do to be supportive (rather than catering), is a start. Don, a polyamorous man who has had difficulty in several relationships, realizes that he has a gifted brain (though I am the first person who referred to him in this positive way) and that his behaviors cause problems for others as well as himself. In a new relationship with a poly woman who has another partner, Don came for help in understanding how to make this relationship work. Here is the story Don told me.

> Jessie is the first partner who understands me because she was diagnosed as a kid with ADD. I know I have bad habits. Ever since I was a kid—yes, I was diagnosed with ADHD and given Ritalin. It made me jumpy! It's speed, for crying out loud. Other drugs made me foggy. Nothing really helped and I got put into special classes. I've done some reading and I don't think I'm

stupid now, but I sure did then. My self-esteem was in the dumper. My mom was beside herself, cleaning up after me and I always forgot things! Homework at school, soccer shoes on the field, you name it. That's why I did poorly. The only thing I was good at was art. My teacher was amazed, but it wasn't hard, I could just—paint! Draw anything. I won a prize at the school art show. Well, sports, I was good too, got on the team but these things wouldn't "get me anywhere in life," was all I ever heard. Good thing I got a computer in high school— that's what got me into tech jobs.

Well, anyways, fast forward. I've been in two poly relationships and in some ways that helped because I didn't have to be perfect everything for one person. At first I was under less emotional pressure but there's too much discussion needed, and sometimes in bed [with partners]—I get antsy, anxious—distracted is what I've been told. Barb [previous partner] knew it was me, not her, and she had David, too, so she'd get better attention from him. Barb said that didn't replace me and her being close. They both got sick of me being late, forgetting things. I couldn't pull my weight in the house or be counted on with Barb. But now, Jessie is like me—so, great, the blind leading the blind, right? But she got help before and figured out all these tools for remembering and organizing. She's learned things and she knows that I can too. She helped me realize I can learn to function better, but I need help and tools. I actually have two calendars now—the phone and reminders on that—and a kitchen white board calendar. Jess and I go over it every night. We eat together except when she's out with Jodie. Daily life is better. I have to struggle to remember the "systems" for staying organized, as Jessie calls 'em, but I'm better than I ever have been. I still have a hellova time with intimacy, is what Jessie says. The sex anxiety hasn't changed and I don't know what to do and I just check out. I feel better about myself, though. Like EVERYthing I do isn't wrong. That's how I got the confidence to come here [to a sex therapist].

Don and Jessie worked with sensate focus intimacy and mindfulness exercises for a few months (Masters & Johnson, 1970; Masters, Johnson, & Kolodny, 1994; Weiner & Avery-Clark, 2017). They each reported learning tools to connect and stay in the moment during sex. Don got a handle on the automatic anxiety (performance anxiety) that had plagued him throughout his life during sexual encounters. As partners, these mindfulness-in-intimacy skills helped them heal from the many disappointing sexual episodes they had experienced, and develop a new way of accessing sensual and emotional intimacy. Sensate focus is a staple in the training of sex therapists, but not in general therapy. A referral to a certified sex therapist is required. Sensate focus can be applied to a myriad of sexual issues and problems. When Masters and Johnson developed this treatment protocol for sex therapy, the term *mindfulness* had not yet been invented, but we know now that sensate focus is mindfulness training for couples, applied to sexual intimacy, and among other uses, teaches the skill of paying attention in the moment while being physical with one's partner.

Remove Fault and Blame

Information about brains is helpful. Personal healing can take place with understanding that all problems and behaviors have not been due to deliberate bad choices or mistakes, that improvement is possible with help and new skills. Individuals cannot connect and pay attention when they are internally bashing themselves—or when others are bashing them and in pain due to this person's behavior. Don improved personally and in daily living. The skills Jessie shared with him and the support provided to one another suggest ways a therapist can help gifted brain people (if they don't have their own "Jessie").

Help Redesign Attention-Demanding Activities

Accessing emotions and expressing them appropriately (if at all), and paying focused attention for longer than a sentence, are often problems for the gifted brain person. Emotional conversations, sex, and long meetings with partners are examples of things that may cause a feeling of being overwhelmed. I have found these interventions helpful: Short frequent talks effectively replace long meetings or spontaneous drama-filled conversations. A few deep breaths and deliberately relaxing the body before trying to talk or connect can help calm the nervous system. Touching while sitting together, hugs, and cuddle time without pressure may be helpful in maintaining intimate connection; this helps sexual encounters feel less sudden and requires less attention shifting. If sex is one of the main stressors brought to the therapist, and this issue is fraught with anxiety, attention, connection, or function issues that do not clear up easily, refer this person and possibly all partners to a certified sex therapist.

Scheduling Quality Time

Scheduling time with each partner is usually considered a necessity in CNM. For some, anticipating time together is pleasurable. For others, planned time can cause pressure and anticipatory anxiety about the requirement to give and receive focused attention at will. Among those who have attention imbalance I have heard some clients say they can be intensely present during sex, while others express being very anxious, causing them to "check out." Choosing to focus attention is not under their control. Without this skill, focus is erratic and easily derailed. It is noticeable to partners when these individuals "disappear," during sex or otherwise. Scheduling time (see Chapter 7) is a necessary start to teaching connection skills, which include mindfulness and deliberately focusing attention with a partner. Scheduling time, and being able to *connect* at that time, are, however, two different requirements and two separate sets of skills.

Denise and Alonzo are clients who exemplify this issue. Denise told me in a follow-up session:

> You know, 'lonzo would not seem to be with me, even though we were having sex. I'll never forget the time we were in bed, making love, at least I thought we were. He suddenly got up and left the room without saying anything. I thought he had to pee or something, although he didn't say anything, he just left. I was startled but figured he'd be right back. After a while when he was still gone, I got out of bed and went to find him. He was at the kitchen table on the computer in his boxers! I was shocked. I said: "What are you doing? We were right in the middle of making love?!!" He looked at me in surprise and said, "We were?" Oh my God, I thought. He doesn't even realize how checked out he is!

Clinicians can help gifted brain persons learn to deliberately prepare for quality togetherness by teaching mindfulness (or referring them elsewhere to learn). Sensate focus can be transformative of many issues related to intimacy and sexuality. General mindfulness training can be self-taught or learned in many settings, including with some therapists, and helps partners learn to center and calm themselves, and to bring their attention to chosen activities, both alone and with someone else. Abilities increase with practice. In other words, even gifted brain persons can learn to be deliberately mindful when they *put their minds to it.* Almost anyone can learn to pay better attention. Alonzo needed to start at step number one: awareness of his own brain and behavior.

Learning Mindfulness in CNM

There are many ways that multiple partners can learn and use mindfulness techniques. Individuals of the gifted brain type especially need to learn it. (Of course they may need help remembering to do it and what the instructions are.) Clients can seek meditation groups, instructors, or therapists online or in person, who teach stress and anxiety reduction through various mindfulness techniques and activities. Books, CDs, videos, and podcasts abound on teaching meditation, providing guided meditations, and living a mindful daily life. Here are ideas from my CNM clients:

- Partners, families, and groups meditate together, or attend meditation groups.
- Take a class on meditation or mindfulness if individuals or partners have difficulty learning and maintaining practices on their own.
- Journal about feelings for clarity and relief.
- Prayer by any name is a form of meditation.
- Connect with nature. Nature calms the mind and nervous system. Really take time to smell the roses.
- Movement—whatever works for you. Moving the body mindfully moves the mind and relieves stress. Many types of exercise can be done mindfully, or are meditative in nature and engender complete focus.

- Listen to music. This can be combined with movement!
- Make a list of positive things to do, and really focus attention on one, when a partner is with someone else (rather than allowing anxious or jealous thoughts to take over).
- Clean the house mindfully. For example, explore the bubbles of the dish soap: the sound they make, how they smell, what happens when grease gets in. This approach can be applied to any daily activity.
- Read about Tantric spirituality and sex. Several "beginner" exercises use breathing, focus, and simple connection techniques to help partners connect in the moment.

There's an app for that! If people find it easier to work with technology, several websites offer a low-cost membership with anytime access to guided meditations from 10–60 minutes, including with focus on specific issues such as sleep, creativity, happiness, anxiety, general calming, and relationships. YouTube offers guided meditations as short as 1 minute. Google "mindfulness activities" and see what comes up!

I find it relieving that we can live only one moment at a time with our physical beings. This is a fact that our minds cannot deny. We cannot be in two places at once. Only our minds go forward and back in time, taking our focus away from *here and now*. Since we cannot go forward or back in time physically, ongoing stress is caused when our mind isn't staying where our bodies are. I teach clients a technique I use myself that I call "just drive." Whatever you are doing, *just do that*. Obviously driving is a good example of when we must pay attention to what we are doing. Even if our minds wander, we'd better refocus on the road. Remind yourself that you cannot physically be anywhere but here right now. Take a few slow, deep breaths. Relax the shoulders. When you get to where you are going, then you will be there and you will deal with it, but for now, *just drive*. Just eat. Just enjoy the beauty of nature on this walk. Just be with this partner, here and now.

Everything happens in the moment, whether it's being connected and paying attention, or experiencing a moment full of problems. We have to deal with things in the moment, when problems or joys are actually happening. Training the mind to stay with the body in the present is a skill that supports contentment and richness in each relationship.

Life is every moment strung together and always being created. The question is, how are your moments? Mindfulness teaches us to answer that question and supports us in creating moments of truly receiving attention, in paying full attention to those we love—however many loves there are.

References

Baer, R. A. (2003). Mindfulness training as a clinical intervention: A conceptual and empirical review. *Clinical Psychology: Science and Practice, 10*, 125–143.
Deninger, J., Lazar, S., & Vago, D. (2016, March 8). Now and Zen: How mindfulness

can change your brain and improve your health. Seminar, Harvard Medical School. Boston, MA.

Greenberg, T., & Alexis, R. (2011). Nurturing mindfulness in children and youth: Current state of research. *Child Development Perspectives*, doi: 10.1111/j.1750-8606.2011.00215.x.

Hoge, E. A., Bui, E., Palitz, S. A., Schwartz, N. R., Owens, M. E., Johnston, J. M., (2017). The effect of mindfulness meditation training on biological acute stress responses in generalized anxiety disorder. *Psychiatry Research*, doi: http://dx.doi.org/10.1016/j.psychres.2017.01.006

Kabat-Zinn, J. (1979/2013). *Full catastrophe living: Using the wisdom of your body and mind to face stress, pain, and illness* (rev. ed.). New York: Bantam Books.

Kemeny, M. E. (2016, October). The immune system: The mind-body connection: Who gets sick and who stays well. *Department of Psychiatry*, University of California, San Francisco. Seminar sponsored by Institute for Brain Potential. Sacramento, CA.

Kleinplatz, P., Ménard, A., Paquet, M., Paradis, N., Campbell, M., Zuccarino, D., (2009). The components of optimal sexuality: A portrait of "great sex." *The Canadian Journal of Human Sexuality, 18* (1–2), 1–13.

Masters, W. H. & Johnson, V. E. (1970). *Human sexual inadequacy.* New York: Bantam Books.

Masters, W. H., Johnson, V. E., & Kolodny, R. (1994). *Heterosexuality* (pp. 25–41). New York: HarperCollins.

Merriam-Webster. Attention. Retrieved April 7, 2017, from www.merriam-webster.com/dictionary/attention

Merriam-Webster. Mindfulness. Retrieved April 7, 2017, from www.merriam-webster.com/dictionary/mindfulness

Rock, C. (1999). Bigger and blacker. *Home Box Office (HBO) presentation*, released July 10.

Siegel, D. (2007). *The mindful brain.* New York: W.W. Norton & Company, Inc.

Weiner, L., & Avery-Clark, C. (2017). *Sensate focus in sex therapy.* New York: Routledge.

Case Excerpt: Sherry, Barry, and Shepherd

Sherry and Barry are therapy clients who agreed to share their story. Each is in their mid-thirties. They have lived together for 4 years, they own a home, and have no children. Neither has been previously married and both have had relatively short-term relationships in the past. Barry is finishing an architecture degree. They share many interests and activities that they each find important, including supporting each other's careers, and visions of being together into the future. They view themselves as primary partners with an expanded sexual agreement and a long-term future. They may not fulfill that view; difficulties are discussed at the end.

Sherry consulted me in a state of distress. Her health care practice was just getting off the ground and she was working too many hours. Problems with colleagues and a stressful commute were taking a toll on her health. She had frequent migraines and kept getting colds. She heaped worry about financial stability and *what ifs* upon herself. What if this set of professional partners didn't work out; what would happen to her entire career? Would she have to relocate? And a cascade of other fears. Compounding this list are concerns about her CNM relationship with her primary partner, Barry, and her secondary partner, Shepherd.

When Sherry and Barry met, part of the attraction was their mutual general view on nonmonogamy: "As long as it's honest and safe." Sherry and Barry are glad to have in each other a partner who agrees about consensual nonmonogamy. Neither has had much experience carrying it out, especially in the context of a primary relationship. When originally dating, Sherry and Barry agreed that having the option for more open sexual expression would help their relationship continue to be exciting.

Barry and Sherry both feel that exclusive sexuality is not a hinge to a relationship commitment and can cause pressure, when all needs must be met by just the two partners. "Sex shouldn't be the deal maker or breaker of a relationship." They know it is more than sex that makes a relationship strong and long term.

Sherry has a pleasant family of origin background, but she lived in a small town with few friends. She has one older sibling who was not in Sherry's life much, then went off to college. Sherry was bullied in school and feels that experience causes her to have insecurities and abandonment issues. One of the girls who bullied her had been her best friend for many years then turned on her. Sherry feels this permanently traumatized her and causes her to feel unsafe in relationships.

Before Sherry came into his life, no partner had worked out for Barry longer than six months. He accepts responsibility for having trouble with emotional connection. Sometimes he admits this is due to a past which includes family abuse and other problems. He also attributes his relationship difficulties to being "a nerd"—a super intellectual who likes things neat and orderly, "which emotions are not." He agrees that this is something he needs to work on with Sherry.

Barry wants an open relationship in part because of these problems with long-term connection. His idea of *open* is to have periodic, brief, relatively unknown secondary partners. Sherry thinks Barry may be trying to learn better overall social relating with Shonda, a woman he has seen more than a few times and with whom he maintains periodic contact. Barry does not feel a "connection" with Shonda; he states she's a friend with whom he shares a few interests, and sex occasionally. Sherry is comfortable with Barry's relationship with Shonda and does not feel a need to meet or know much about her.

Barry's casual and periodic relationship with Shonda is typical of his personality. He is socially withdrawn and awkward and has difficulty with emotions and intimacy. This is partly why he has trouble understanding and accepting the in-depth relationship that Sherry developed with Shepherd.

Conflict about CNM arrangements arose when Sherry learned that Barry's definition of *open*—anonymity and brevity—does not work for her. She tried going on a date for casual sex with a man Barry knows, but Sherry was very uncomfortable. In order to be sexual with someone, she needs to have an ongoing connection, which takes her some time to build. Sherry does not need many people in her life and becomes bonded with the few she has.

Barry joined many therapy sessions. At other times Sherry came alone. She explained that she first scheduled a consult because she and Barry had started arguing more, and she knew that her high level of emotion drove Barry from being able to engage in effective communication. She had also developed a more in-depth relationship with Shepherd, who is a friend of both Sherry and Barry. Her former friendship with Shepherd developed into an intimate and sexual one that is not the type of partnership originally agreed upon between Sherry and Barry.

Now that Barry struggles with Sherry's secondary relationship, she feels insecure about his commitment to her. Intertwined with this is one of the issues Barry and Sherry have trouble with, disclosure: how much to tell one another about their outside relationships and dates.

Sherry has experimented with how much to tell Barry about what she does with her "second," Shepherd, or even whether to disclose when she is seeing him. Barry says he "doesn't like ambiguity" and claims he worries less if he knows whether or not Sherry and Shepherd will be having sex on a given visit.

Sherry's experience is that this is not so. She observed that they both have more stress and tension when either of them shares more information about their respective other dates. She also feels uncomfortable herself sharing intimate details about partners.

Barry views Shepherd as—*it's just Shepherd*—because Shepherd has been a common friend for so long. Further, Barry states:

> I don't take Shepherd very seriously as a partner for Sherry. We've known him for years and he's not a very pleasant guy. He can be rude. He doesn't take care of his health—he smokes and drinks! He's the opposite of Sherry.

Sherry didn't seek out Shepherd. He was a friend who, over time, developed an intimate connection with Sherry, despite those shortcomings listed by Barry. They all used to meet socially; it was unexpected that Sherry and Shepherd became close. Sherry does not have future plans with Shepherd nor does she view him as a possible full-time permanent partner. Yet Sherry finds the emotional support and laid-back friendship she shares with Shepherd vital to her own survival.

Barry claims, "If it was any other man," he'd feel more respectful and be able to feel more "separate." He accepts and verbally admits that he does not provide Sherry with the emotional and relaxed connection she often needs, and he understands that this is why Sherry needs Shepherd. But it makes him feel inadequate.

Another issue that catalyzed Sherry to seek help is time. Barry recently finished months of school, on top of his job as a manager, which had left Sherry often alone. She and Shepherd therefore had time together, and this supported the development of their relationship. Now that Barry has more time to share, he expects more of Sherry. Meantime Sherry had established a schedule, including her long work hours, during the months when Barry was less available. Sherry has now made adjustments to share more time with Barry, but she is still working long hours and needs to have certain times with Shepherd.

Barry complains that Sherry is at Shepherd's house a lot and could instead be at home. Sherry clarifies that she does come home, usually tired and stressed. When she needs a relaxing, or at least not stressful, evening, or some support because she's feeling bad, Barry can't seem to connect or relax with Sherry, or they argue. Sherry then goes to Shepherd's where his roommates (a girlfriend of Sherry's and her husband) may also be present. Sherry is able to relax and, if upset, gets support from both Shepherd and their friends.

Sherry says that even though she goes to Shepherd's house, she and Shepherd get little private time together and can't routinely show their affection. Sherry explained that she and Shepherd have to be "secretive" despite the CNM agreement. Friends in the social circle frequented by all three partners might not understand or maintain discretion if they knew about the open relationship. Shepherd's roommates do not know the real situation either. Sherry hangs out at their house and finds it relaxing and laid back, but unless the roommates are not home, Shepherd and Sherry have very little private time and "can't even hold hands."

"Unless it's Tuesday mornings when [the roommates] are out, or we go to a hotel, we're never alone," explains Sherry. Barry, she feels, makes a mountain out of a molehill with regard to the time she has with Shepherd.

Barry will not be back in school for a few months. He's been voicing his excitement that he and Sherry will have lots of time together now. She wants that also, but has to find a way to manage her own busy work schedule—which has not changed just because Barry is temporarily out of school—and the time she has come to need with Shepherd.

Sherry talks about some of the good things going on with Shepherd. She explains that Shepherd has shortcomings but is "emotionally available and not afraid of my feelings." He helps her work through anxiety. She observed gladly that Shepherd is doing things to take better care of himself physically, due to her influence. She not only feels supported, but effective—as if she matters.

She reports that Barry, too, has been working hard, following through on anything discussed in therapy sessions, such as working at kinder, more clear and frequent communication, focusing on Sherry and himself together, using thought-stopping and positive self-talk to battle jealousy. Everyone involved cares and is trying.

Barry's outside partner, Shonda, while not a deeply significant relationship, helps Barry relax and feel that he, too, has "rights" in the CNM relationship structure. He does not have to work on himself particularly with Shonda, so he can just relax, focusing on his personal growth efforts in his primary relationship.

Barry, his attention now returned more to his home life, is struggling to find his emotional place with Sherry. He knows that his blocks against intimacy affect his relationship with Sherry (or anyone) and that this is partly why she seeks solace with Shepherd. Barry is motivated to keep working on himself, but he does spend significant mental time and energy managing jealousy. He also questions his part in Sherry's life.

For several sessions, Barry continues to struggle with feeling left out, jealous, and resentful that Sherry is now *polyamorous* while he, Barry, never wanted that. He wanted only "unimportant" side relationships for both of them.

When I asked what he does exactly to manage his feelings, including jealousy, he explained that he "goes away"—removes his attention (and usually himself) from Sherry so he can think and "organize my emotions." This method has not helped Barry and does not include Sherry in the process of discussing and resolving issues.

Barry declares that intellectually he knows Sherry's secondary partner can't replace him. He knows that Sherry loves him, Barry, that she believes they are together long term, and that he and Sherry are "home." Yet he keenly feels her absence and allows his mind to fill in blanks with overblown scenarios between Sherry and Shepherd. "I know I drive her away—the very thing I'm mad at her for doing [going away]!"

Jealousy is a bear.

Barry describes using calming techniques and positive self-talk to deal with his negative feelings. Yet he still spends hours in absentia from Sherry arguing with his brain. The cognitive behavioral skills he describes are either not working or not being used effectively.

No one can live like that for long. Despite his efforts, his jealousy and distance are apparent. Sherry is bending over backwards—too far—desperately trying to get Barry's love and attention, to "make him feel OK, talk with me." But if Barry can't let in Sherry's love and desire, he cannot be helped by them. Meanwhile Sherry is doing too much for no response, which is contributing to her health issues.

One session Barry announced that he told Sherry he wants to be a "second"— no longer a primary partner with Sherry. She was devastated. Barry was kind about it and realized it hurt and scared Sherry. He spoke and acted in comforting ways. I asked, "What does it mean to you, to be a second? How does that play out? Are you moving out, separating bank accounts. . .?"

Barry explains that nothing would really change. They will continue living together for the time being, sharing finances and "having each other's back." The difference is Barry *feeling* that he could possibly find another primary partner some day. Although he does not come right out and say it, he wants to feel that the way things are now, won't always be. His perspective needs to be that he's not trapped in this relationship where he feels *less than*. "We never made it official, but I guess I just feel now that we don't have *'til death do us part* plans."

I point out that this is partly a perspective change on Barry's part. Even if they thought they knew their future together, no one knows what will actually happen, and at least 50% of people are wrong more than once. Of course, having a commitment into years ahead feels more secure, and many people work to fulfill such a commitment.

Big issues and questions immediately came up and were outlined in Sherry's response. She cried:

> It's when I go to bed, that's the one thing I can count on daily is finally getting into bed with Barry. Will people be coming to the house? I already don't like people we know coming over that often, let alone women you are dating. And will these dates you find know I'm your girlfriend?

Barry did look sad and to comfort Sherry told her, "Until further notice, we're still sleeping in the same bed, and I'm not dating."

I suggested that in practice, their relationship has not changed much. Barry was already allowed to date, and no one ever knows how something will develop. Sherry after all had no idea that Shepherd would become an important partner to her. Barry simply *feels* less trapped and mentally free by placing himself in a different role within the threesome. He can imagine a different life happening later, if this one doesn't work out, i.e., if he never gets a handle on his jealousy.

Barry went on to say:

> We talked about Sherry not seeing Shepherd but despite myself, I don't want that and we both know that wouldn't work. You can't un-love somebody.

I understand how it happened between Sherry and Shepherd, but I never wanted polyamory. I just wanted sexy fun, a way to let off steam and keep steam going with Sherry.

"But casual is just not me!" cried Sherry. "I have to know people to feel comfortable. I wasn't even looking."

Barry is nodding his head and they are holding hands. "I know, I know that's true. I know it's not her fault," he says to me.

Sherry exclaims, looking at Barry and me alternately,

> But I can't make him believe me, how important he is! Shepherd and I never talk about the future. It's the last thing he wants! He's not a good partner for the long term. I don't know what's going to happen, but it's Barry who is my security. You are the main man! We do talk about the future. We have—at least did have—plans.

Barry has assuaged his jealousy by taking away the spoken long-term commitment, the label of "primary." He can't get a handle on his emotions, so they have a handle on him. He wants Sherry but also pushes her away, to feel free of fear of abandonment, of feeling *less than*. The alternative would require Barry to increase his sharing of deep emotions with Sherry, to directly express and receive support for his feelings of low self-esteem. He'd have to *be there* a lot more often emotionally in connection with Sherry. He would need to control his mind and choose behaviors other than isolating and obsessing.

They talk about what they now say to people if their relationship is changing. Anything different? Will Barry introduce or talk about Sherry as his girlfriend or partner?

Barry admits that with some people he'd meet for the first time "on the outside," he might not tell them he has a serious live-in girlfriend.

> I never seek or plan on getting involved long term with people. I always use condoms. I don't tell every outside partner I meet that I'm in a committed relationship because I doubt I will see them seriously [frequently or meaningfully]. When I decided to keep seeing Shonda, even with her, it's casual, she doesn't want more either. We like the same games and books, we have dinner and a little sex fairly infrequently. But her I did tell about Sherry when I realized I wanted to see her more than once or twice.

For now Barry and Sherry continue to live as primary partners, but Barry has taken away his commitment to stay with her for the long term or to necessarily put her first in his life decisions. He discusses the future in ways that might not include her.

Sherry is unable to stop loving either Barry or Shepherd. A big lesson in CNM is that love is not something we own or control. It develops and flows regardless of the organized plans we may make. Like Barry and Sherry, partners may start out with a certain type of "open" in mind, but unexpected depth in some relationships can occur and change everything.

Discussion

At first, this couple demonstrates that their relationship benefits from the CNM arrangements, even though they are each struggling with personal growth, time, and communication. Each has the opportunity to get needs met. They feel close because they share the trust that CNM takes, and their own relationship is not under as much pressure to be the context for everything. Barry, however, does struggle often with feelings of low self-worth and resentment.

Barry works on intimacy and supporting Sherry emotionally, and meanwhile Sherry might have left the relationship had Shepherd not been there for her. At the same time, Shepherd's inability to be a full-time, long-term partner is not a problem; just as Shonda can provide noncommittal support to Barry. All partners do not work together and there are some tough challenges involved. These relationships also support each other and provide positive benefits for each person involved.

Because they actively work on their own relationship, Sherry and Barry demonstrate that the side relationships are not an escape from having to work on their own issues. The secondary partner also helps significantly with personal growth in specific areas. Sherry and Shepherd are a necessary emotional support to one another, enabling each one to do other important personal work, including for Sherry and Barry to keep figuring out how to live together, if possible.

9 Sex and Consensual Nonmonogamy

Introduction

As I was growing up in the 1960s and 1970s my best friend, Ally, had a family who was considered unusual. Ally's father had died and her mother did not remarry. A friend, who was divorced, moved in with her two children. To help with bills, an older friend joined the group. The children called him "Uncle Ralph."

Divorce was barely accepted in those days so Ally's family situation was questioned by some who may have looked askance, but Ally and her family were not dangerously stigmatized. No one seemed to care that much, because the members of Ally's household were not sexual nor romantic together. If they had been, she would have been part of what is now called a "poly family." What's the difference between consensual nonmonogamy (CNM) and family and friends just living together? Sex.

In my experience, responses to the idea of CNM by those who don't know much about it include negative stigmatization, curiosity, fear of complex intimate relationships, or excitement about being "allowed" to have multiple sex partners. Is sex in consensual nonmonogamy so different from sex in consensual monogamy? Is sex the reason people engage in CNM? Sex shared by multiple friends, strangers, and unrelated domestic partners does create questions, complications, and concerns, including:

- Why choose consensual nonmonogamy?
- Are multiple sexual partnerships worth the work?
- Physical health and safer sex
- Emotional safety with multiple sex partners
- Safety in "kinky" sex

Let's examine these questions and concerns.

Why Choose Consensual Nonmonogamy?

Isn't one relationship complicated enough? Oughtn't having sex with one person in a secure relationship be enough for any individual? Many have reported to me about sex within their CNM relationship with phrases such as "it's always interesting"; "the sex is spiritual"; "we all share deep feelings"; "the sex is bonding"; "it's the highest sex of our lives"; and that "multiple partners keep sex from getting boring." *Expanded monogamy* couples (swingers and those in open relationships, see Chapter 3) often tell me that sex within their primary relationship is better because they have a strong bond through sharing an open relationship, and that having sex with outside partners brings more spark and passion to their own primary sexual relationship.

Maintaining an ongoing satisfying sexual relationship in a long-term monogamous agreement is difficult and can create pressure. Sexual interest and activity change for individuals over the lifespan and also within relationships. Being flexible or open with the sexual aspect helps some couples stay together (Orion, 2011). Sharing the responsibility of sex with other partners may provide relief from pressure.

I recall clients, a family, including polyamorous adults, who divided sex nights in the same practical way they divided housecleaning, childcare, and cooking: Those who liked certain tasks most were willing to do more of them. One of the two female partners told me she was once asked if she got jealous sharing the man sexually; and conversely she was asked if sex is the only reason that she is in the relationship. "You've got to be kidding!" she said in my office. "I told them I would so much rather have a good soak in the tub with a book! Let them have at it, I'm glad the sex is not all my responsibility, especially after the packed days I usually have."

My research (Orion, 2008a, 2011) and my clinical experience show that many are compelled into CNM, rather than it being a choice based only on a desire for more sex partners. Sex is not necessarily any better in CNM than in monogamy. Sex is not the only or most important reason reported for involvement in multiple or open relationships. Polyamorous partners get involved because they connect or fall in love, just as with monogamy. Sex is then an expectable or integral component. Some expanded monogamy agreements are founded on a mutual desire or acceptance of two primary partners allowing extra-dyadic relationships that are sexual, but not love-based—"It's just sex." Others may have more than two or three love-based partnerships, which may or may not include sex.

A double study (Conley, Matsick, Moors, & Ziegler, 2017) reveals that many of the self-identified "open" couples include a primary partner who is unavailable—*not present*—such as being in the military, or one partner is unable to engage in the type of sex desired by the other. This research supports the idea that some couples and individuals are compelled into consensual nonmonogamy by factors over which they have no control.

The situation of a partner being "not present" is very common, takes many forms, and can have negative and serious results on intimacy (see Chapter 8). Dr. Marty Klein (2017) writes in his Sexual Intelligence blog (www.martyklein.com/sex-lives-engineers-humans):

> Partner sex [as different from masturbation] requires us to show up. What we do with our hands, mouths, and genitalia is important, but it's overrated. The most important things we do in sex are mental: we do or don't pay

attention, notice the other person, limit our distractibility, communicate our experience moment by moment, whether verbally or nonverbally.

For those activities, however, there is no formula. We can learn to be more present. But it's pointless to try to pretend to be present—even if you think someone really wants that from you.

The difficult part of sex isn't the sexual "function" part—erection, lubrication, orgasm. It isn't the skill part—the perfect handjob, knowing a dozen ways to kiss. For most people, the difficult part is being present.

There are many reasons for not being present, including loss of interest in sex. Lack of desire, or "desire discrepancy" (one partner currently needs more sex than the other) leading to low or no sex between partners, is an issue presented frequently to many therapists and physicians (Orion, 2011). Loss of sexual interest by one partner and not the other is one reason some clients have changed their relationships from monogamous to consensually nonmonogamous. Other reasons may include illness or physical disability of one partner, and personal mental health issues such as depression, attention deficit disorder (see Chapter 8), and post-traumatic stress. (Or, one person falls in love with a second partner, and nobody wants to end any of the relationships.)

Jill and Jack's *don't ask, don't tell* (Orion, 2008a, 2008b, 2011) expanded monogamy marriage is a good example of desire discrepancy. Jill's progressive loss of interest in sex, despite several measures taken by the couple, led them to try consensual nonmonogamy. This couple does not report passion between them, but they do love one another, have a very high commitment level, high trust, and low jealousy. Allowing Jack to have outside partners has been a relief to Jill and to Jack. They report that their CNM arrangement saved their marriage, which has lasted 29 years as of this writing.

A less happy case example includes a couple I call "the reluctant polyamorists." Married for 25 years, desire discrepancy and sexual style differences always impacted Myra and Mitch. Recently Mitch happened to find online an old high school girlfriend, Lana, and met her for coffee. After not seeing her for 30 years, Mitch had no thought or intention of this meeting leading to anything but catching up and possible friendship, but he and Lana experienced a spark and connection that seemed to have remained throughout the years.

Mitch said in a session with me:

> I care about my marriage and love Myra so much that I had given up on sex, there's no other way to say it. Over the last years I'd begun to accept, to think, OK, well I guess that's just not going to be there. I never looked to cheat or thought of finding another wife.

I explained that shutting down one's sexuality can happen when that aspect of an otherwise good relationship isn't there for long enough. Mitch continued:

> That's it. I slowly made myself stop thinking about sex and I figured I may as well accept it than be frustrated all the time. At our age, I thought, security

and caring for each other are most important and that will have to be enough. I figured having no sex must be common for old married couples like us.

Shutting down does not mean removing the sex drive, however, or the aspects of self enlivened by sex. When Mitch met Lana for a simple coffee, the connection that was "just there" woke the sleeping dragon. He told me this story of his experience:

> I didn't mean for this to happen and I was wrong to cheat, because that's where it went. But I felt alive! I hadn't realized how much of myself was part of that sexual shut-down. It's not like Myra would have said yes if I'd asked her first, and I know that I hurt her badly when she guessed I'd been seeing someone, and I admitted it. I keep thinking, I could have, should have, not gone with Lana, but at the same time, I couldn't say no—or say anything. For the first time in years, I felt alive with something genuine I hadn't realized I missed. It's not just sex. Lana could never replace Myra, but we [Mitch and Lana] have a real connection. Now, I can't honestly tell Myra I'd be able to stay away from Lana, or that I can do without that part of me that I have back. I still love Myra. I can't choose one over the other, like they want. I wish I could! I've been confused and miserable about the effect of my actions on all of us. But these feelings won't go away! If I hadn't experienced really loving both women, I wouldn't believe it was possible.

Mitch moved to a separate apartment alone, but did not divorce Myra who still calls Mitch daily. The two meet frequently to keep up the house, see family, or talk. Mitch sees Lana several times a week and has supported her through a medical procedure with a lengthy recovery. The women know about each other but do not want a negotiated sharing situation. Each is waiting (for 2 years now) for Mitch to choose one woman or the other. Mitch keeps thinking he'll get "clear" or "get over" one of them, but he does not. He continues to be honest with both women about the fact that he does see both of them, and that he can't choose, which is why he lives alone.

Though the women have not met and would not willingly choose the idea of sharing Mitch, they are actually doing so, reluctantly in a consensually nonmonogamous relationship—and managing, albeit with difficulty. Now Myra is dating a new man (being honest that she's still legally married) because she feels that's fair, which adds one more to a group of people compelled into CNM.

Are Multiple Sexual Partnerships Worth the Work?

Conley et al. (2017) compared various relationship factors, including sexual satisfaction, of monogamous participants to the same factors of partners in three types of consensual nonmonogamy: swinging, open marriage, and polyamory. "Notably, means on all scales indicate generally high levels of relational adjustment in both groups." Both types of relationships show general satisfaction and no differences in levels of commitment. Monogamous and CNM respondents reported similar depths of passionate love.

Sex and jealousy can go hand in hand. One presumption about monogamy is that maintaining the single intimate relationship prevents jealousy (see Chapter 5). Having worked with numerous jealous monogamous clients, I know that presumption to be untrue. In the Conley et al. study, jealousy scores were lower, and trust higher, in CNM, as compared to monogamy. Those in CNM may be predisposed to higher trust levels and less jealousy, or they have learned skills and developed personally to achieve these results. (The researchers point out that the difference in trust scores between monogamous and CNM respondents is not huge—both groups revealed high levels of trust for partners.)

Interesting is that those in "open relationships" reported lowest levels of passionate love compared to other groups (Conley et al., 2017). What I term *expanded monogamy* (see Chapter 3) includes swingers, who do not seek love-based liaisons, and couples who allow each spouse to have extramarital partners. These may score in the Conley et al. study as the least adjusted relationally, because this group may have rules wherein a partner can have *sex* with others, but not *love* others. Since it is not possible to control who we love, aptly demonstrated by Mitch and supported by much literature and research in the field of sexology, following this rule of "sex but no love" can be difficult (see Chapter 4). Conley et al. (2017) state:

> The fact that the polyamorous groups reported greater relational outcomes on most measures could indicate that the polyamorous style of relationship—in which both sexual intimacy and emotional intimacy with multiple people are allowed—is particularly effective. If one of the purposes of sex is emotional intimacy . . . perhaps it is more difficult for an individual to be satisfied in one relationship while attempting to suppress emotional and romantic feelings for others with whom that individual is sexual, as is expected in [some] open relationships and swinging.

It's also likely that some in polyamorous relationships choose them because such individuals are suited to high communication and sharing levels—and have the skills and temperaments to make poly work.

One assumption often made by therapists and others who are unfamiliar with CNM realities is that if a primary couple has outside partners, that primary couple must be sexually unsatisfied with one another. According to my experience and research (Orion, 2007, 2008a, 2011), this is sometimes true; however, Conley et al. (2017) report that most expanded monogamy couples in their study:

> appeared to be very pleased with their primary partners vis-à-vis their other partner . . . They reported more satisfaction, trust, commitment, and passionate love in their primary than their secondary relationship. They also had more jealous cognitions in their primary relationship than in their secondary . . .

This is information that "secondary" partners may wish to heed!

Physical Health and Safer Sex

Sex has always been potentially deadly. I was a teen in the 1970s, a decade which is sometimes referred to (at least by me!) as the golden age of sex. Never before had sex been safer: the pill had been invented, giving women control over pregnancy; abortion became legal. Socially, loving the one you were with was accepted. There was no HIV/AIDS, and venereal diseases that had killed so many in the past were curable with an injection in a physician's office.

Of course, a myriad of other less-discussed infections and viruses are passed via sexual contact. I find that many adults today have little knowledge of sexual health beyond the scary afflictions that make the news media. Facts and myths may also be dangerously mixed up in any given person's lexicon. This is important to address with clients.

Family planning remains an issue. More sexual partners can still lead to pregnancy! I find that CNM clients have thought about and are more careful with regard to safer sex, including pregnancy prevention, than are monogamous clients. This may be especially true for those who cheat. If one takes a trip to the drugstore before cheating, it's clearly premeditated and may derail the liaison. In my clinical experience, alcohol and drug use are often involved as well when cheating occurs, impairing good decision-making with regard to safety and relationship values. A study by Conley, Moors, Ziegler, and Karathanasis (2012) finds that CNM partners are more conscious of and consistent with condom use and other aspects of safe sex than are monogamous partners who cheat. "A growing body of research finds that many partners who have made monogamy agreements cheat, and that when they do, they are less likely to practice safe sex than CNM partners" (Lehmiller, 2015).

I find that safer sex is one of the first issues to be discussed among all types of CNM partners. It is important to clarify agreements and how these are carried out, especially if clients are new to the CNM lifeway. Make referrals to certified sex educators and physicians if appropriate. Therapists can generally discuss physical health with regard to sex and encourage healthy practices, but a certified sexologist and a physician are needed to go beyond general knowledge and advice. The term *safer sex* has come to have a mainstream meaning of using condoms at all times, unless one is strictly monogamous (and knows one's partner also is). With CNM, this general definition may not be as easily applied.

I used to give talks to high school and college students about sex and drugs. Information presented through the years at scientific sexuality organizations about the risk-taking practiced by students and older adults expanded and clarified the definition in my talks of safe sex.

In CNM situations, including more than two consistent partners where commitments are desired, certain actions need to take place. When any two people decide to maintain a sexual relationship, or whenever a new partner comes into the situation, both partners of the new person ought to be tested for all types of sexually transmitted diseases and organisms. New partners use condoms until test results are returned negative. If a new partner enters the group, those in the established partnership use condoms *with the new person* until results are returned. Even if lab reports show no red flags, to be really safe get tested once again in 6 months. If that second test is also fine, then condoms can be discontinued as long as within the partner group, everyone is exclusive sexually (known as "polyfidelitous" in polyamory circles, see Chapter 3).

Partners may decide on additional safeguards and various rules regarding safer sex practices, but a straightforward discussion does need to take place. I have had upset clients because someone got herpes or discovered a partner did not use a condom with another person. Often declared is, "Everyone knows what safe sex is, I didn't think we had to spell it out!"

But spelled out it must be. "Everyone" does not think the same way, and I've heard many people say they "know" that the new partner is safe and trustworthy so they didn't use a condom. Maybe that's true. Every individual's sexual activity may affect other people even unknown to them, but clearly each person in a CNM situation has more than personal health and safety to make decisions about. Some people need reminding that their actions affect more than just their own body and mind.

If the CNM arrangement is swinging or expanded monogamy, in which various partners come and go, the use of condoms or dental dams with all outside partners at all times is ideal for safer sex. If someone is unsure about a primary partner's consistency with condom use, this can be a source of contention brought to the therapy office. I can think of only so many choices, other than abstaining from all fluid-passing sexual activities: The primary couple uses condoms also, and it may be wise to get tested every 6 months; or they create a contract, that they might sign together in a session, to both be diligent with condom use outside their own relationship. This requires both partners to trust each other, and may require further exploration as to why they don't, if trust is an issue.

Some polyamorous partners I have worked with feel that condoms interfere with physical and spiritual energy flow during sex. Others may have allergies to latex. Animal skin condoms are not as protective. Helping people with clarity regarding safer sex may not include what the therapist thinks is best, or what the Centers for Disease Control and Prevention recommend. Like any other charged topic, partners may need help discussing and clarifying what safe sex is and how each person must behave with regard to sexual health. If partners differ on what they want to do, I personally recommend following what is known to be the most preventative set of actions. Through moderated discussion, partners may come up with compromises or less comprehensive rules that work for them—limiting sexual activities to those that don't pass bodily fluids (other than saliva) is one example. A clear discussion is necessary of physical health, including a reminder that someone might get pregnant. If partners show clarity and consensus in their decisions and practices, then the therapist can move on.

Emotional Safety with Multiple Sex Partners

Emotional safety is partly about consent in sex, in CNM agreements (see Chapter 4), and in practices of disclosure inside and outside partnerships (see Chapter 6). The terms *safety* and *consent* need clarification and discussion.

Sexual consent must be made by human adults of legal age, which varies some by state and era. Know the law in your area (and the current era). Consent to sex (or relationship agreements) can be reviewed or withdrawn at any time if a person becomes uncomfortable. This is especially important for teenagers to understand, but we provide virtually no realistic and useful information about sex and relationships to young people (or adults) in this country. In consensual nonmonogamy, it's about comprehensive informed consent: basic knowledge of all partners by all partners, and spoken agreements by all involved, whether or not all partners have met or know each other personally.

Individuals' issues can impact the consent process, just as in any relationship. When communicating to reach consent, "Therapists may see clients whose relationships reflect manipulation, dishonesty, or other dysfunctional patterns that are no more representative of healthy [consensual nonmonogamy] than they are of healthy monogamy" (cited in Weitzman and Davidson, 2010).

Therapists help CNM partners with negotiation and communication skills to reach non-coerced consent. Each individual and set of partners must undergo self-assessment, experimentation with plans and agreements, more self-assessment, discussion, and probable re-negotiation and "tweaking" of plans.

Some CNM clients try various arrangements and agreements in an attempt to feel safe and secure. They may not be successful in creating plans that prevent feelings of insecurity, regardless of what they and their partners try. This occurrence leads me to examine two possibilities: first, that the individual has growth to do with regard to personal sense of security in the world and in relationships; second, CNM may not be the relationship format for them, even if they agree with it. Some individuals do not have a self-esteem level nor sense of personal security that allows them to be successful at CNM (or possibly any relationship), without personal growth and healing.

Therapists must discern between personal perceptions and issues with feeling secure, and CNM arrangements and relationships presenting the challenge. What does it mean to *feel* safe? This means that one's brain *perceives* no danger, whether real in the moment or manufactured by the brain. According to my training and experience, as well as recent brain science, nearly all anxiety is caused by prior experiences and trauma (Gentry, 2016). Unless we are actually in the woods and there's a big bear, we are not in fact, in danger *this moment*. So we are safe. Most of us, if asked, could not deny that we are safe right now. If you are reading this, chances are you are not in immediate danger. So what is meant by emotional safety in CNM relationships? The same thing meant in any relationship—one trusts that partners will not be hurtful by being abusive, breaking commitments, or falling out of love.

How can partners know whether that will happen? They can't. CNM partners have to develop trust with more partners and have a stable level of personal confidence. Trust of another can develop in part through how a partner behaves: Are promises and commitments followed through? Are conflicts handled without verbal or physical abuse? Do partners show their love through word and deed? These actions indicate that a partner is generally trustworthy and safe.

Safe may not be an accurate word to use here. Viktor Frankl said, "Between stimulus and response there is a space. In that space is our power to choose our response. In our response lies our growth and our freedom." In CNM where more partners are involved who can have or cause problems, it may be helpful for each person to understand the difference between personal perceptions of safety and what are actual, immediate threats to any of the relationships involved.

Security may be a more helpful term than safety. Emotional security is dependent upon each person's internal state of security. In multiple relationships, there are many triggers to insecurity, anxiety, and feelings of perceived threat. How can partners act—respond to stimuli—and what can be communicated to create and protect a sense of security? The feeling that things will remain safe and that nobody will be hurt? All partners may want such assurance, especially in CNM relationships which inherently require sharing emotions and time with multiple partners, but there is no absolute assurance for anyone. We cannot predict the future and there is much in life over which one has no control. What we can learn to control is our response to what happens— how we use that space between— and how we handle our perceptions of insecurity. Partners can develop interpersonal behaviors that are trustworthy.

Safety in "Kinky" Sex

According to Lane (2015), in a review in the *New Yorker* magazine, *Fifty Shades of Grey* by E.L. James has sold over one hundred million copies. This book about a couple who engages in bondage and sadomasochism (BDSM) has made the topic of this form of kinky sex popular. The book and ensuing film, however, are not scientific sources of information and are unlikely to represent all people who engage in this form of sexuality. As a sexologist, I know that historically in this culture, sadomasochism has been negatively misunderstood, including in therapeutic communities.

Due to standard lack of training in sexual science, many therapists may feel uncomfortable and unprepared to discuss sex at all with clients, especially activities that may be viewed as non-mainstream. Clients may or may not feel comfortable bringing up sexual issues in therapy. There is unlikely more kinky sex among CNM practitioners than in the general population, although I know of no studies with data on that question. I have found some crossover with kinky sex and CNM so I am discussing this particular sexual interest here.

It is not uncommon to find that "alternative" sex practices are enjoyed by people who are also in alternative types of relationships. From a little spanking to full out dungeons, some form of traditionally labeled BDSM is often also referred to as "kinky sex." I do not try to define "kinky" because I have heard it used to describe various sexual attitudes and activities, and I do not know if there is a definitive use of the term. Maybe it means anything but "vanilla" sex (and we then must ask, what is vanilla?). I'm using "kinky" to mean some form of so-called bondage/sadomasochism, which I believe is important for clinicians to be aware of. These activities may be practiced by any client, but a percentage of my CNM clients specifically formed a multiple partnership because of involvement with kinky sex. One of a couple has kinky interests and the other doesn't, so the relationship was opened to allow for sexual differences; or three or more partners joined in part because of their complementary kinky interests.

Kinky sex is an interest that may impact relationships in specific ways, but it is not considered a problem, nor unhealthy, unless it is carried out unsafely. Clinicians may be able to assess safety, or whether kinky practices are intertwined with other relationship problems. If sexually related problems are not solvable with general therapy approaches, referral to a qualified, certified sex therapist is necessary. (This is true for all sexual issues from erectile dysfunction to sexual pain to low desire or problems with orgasm and many more.)

Kleinplatz and Moser (2006) reveal that partners who regularly practice kinky sex are safer and they communicate better than was previously understood. BDSM partners often discuss well-thought-out scenarios, and have a "safe" word that is a signal to truly stop a particular activity. A high level of trust is developed between partners. A misconception that anyone wishing to be on either side of such activities must have abuse in their past is shown to be false. In short, many "normal" people in every kind of relationship might be involved in BDSM (or other forms of kinky sex). A positive benefit is that BDSM partners have communication skills they use in their sex lives, which may be transferable to other areas of relationships where discussion is difficult. If clients discuss how they communicate about their kinky sex, skills may become visible to the clinician that the partners had not thought of using more widely.

When carried out with respected safe words and communication, "kinky sex" is neither abusive nor dangerous. I was present at a 2006 conference of the American Association of Sex Educators, Counselors, and Therapists when Moser, a physician, pointed out that many seriously injured patients come to his office for medical help, who sustained injures from accepted American sports activities, such as boxing and football. These sports are applauded and injuries are expected. A person in the audience asked if Dr. Moser has patients who practice BDSM. "Yes," he replied, "they come to my office for the same reasons anyone else does—they have the flu, to treat their high blood pressure or diabetes—not because of injuries sustained during kinky sex."

If CNM partners are into kinky sex, this may be a resource for discussion in the therapy office and between partners. Sue is a client who stopped seeing a prospective couple because of how they treated her. The wife of a prospective sex exchange couple wanted Sue as a third partner for herself and her husband. This couple was into BDSM, which Sue had never tried. She met with them casually for coffee and then dinner to find out more and to see if they were all comfortable together. They seemed compatible as a group, but the husband then spoke with Sue individually about sexual activities he wanted her to try with him and his wife. Sue was willing, but when the wife heard that her husband had discussed these activities with Sue, she angrily told Sue that such activities had strict rules and were reserved for herself and her husband. Essentially this is a boundaries issue, not one of safety, but someone like Sue who is not familiar with kinky sex may not know how to play it safe—emotionally or physically—when BDSM activities get underway.

Another female client came to me because she had been raped by a man who practiced BDSM. She was familiar with these practices, and at first was fine in the situation. Further, the man was someone with whom she'd had several dates, including kinky sex. One evening the man probably put Rohipnol in her drink, as she later found herself half-conscious and receiving a beating to which she had not consented. He also did not stop when she remembered her safe word and used it. She was extremely traumatized, and it took weeks for her bruises to disappear. I share this story because this is not safe, consensual sex of any kind. This man used kinky interests as an excuse; he was also impaired and out of control himself by drug abuse that my client had been unaware of.

If you find yourself with CNM clients who are "kinky," it is important to determine that everyone involved does feel safe. Are they going along with BDSM (or any sex) only because they want to please a partner? Or because they are afraid to lose a partner? Is there a feeling of obligation but not personal enjoyment?

Another issue may be that roles played out in the bedroom may not stay in the bedroom and could be part of larger problems partners are experiencing. Lianne came to me with issues in her expanded monogamy marriage, partly related to her BDSM practices. She is a good example of a client who presents problems that are reflected in her sex life, but also involve several other personal and relational difficulties. In Lianne's consult, she presented the following:

> I'm always the dom (dominant role partner in BDSM sex). Corey is always the submissive, which has become our daily lives, too. I am outgoing and I enjoy managing things and making decisions. He'd rather just work, and go along with whatever I have planned. Not that I don't ask him if he wants to go running or to the movies, I mean sometimes he says no, he's not a complete noodle. But I'm a person, too, not just a dom. Sometimes I need him to be more assertive, to initiate things, to reach out to support me or show me love that isn't sex. The only exception, when he's not mostly submissive, is when he gets mad! It doesn't happen often but really, that's not what I mean by assertive! Julie is our third, she plays with us sometimes and we've become friends. She doesn't live with us, but she's a dom, too, and she sees what I'm talking about with Corey. It's like he always hides his emotions and plays that sub [submissive] card. Over time, I've lost my sense of safety with him because I don't know when he'll get mad, and because I can't count on him to be a strong supporter when I need that.

I must reiterate that there is a lack of training for therapists and physicians in how to assess and treat sexual issues, beyond an initial determination. Most of the CNM clients I have seen consult me for reasons other than or in addition to sex problems. When sex is the topic, it is most often about loss of desire or connection with one partner or another. This is also the most common complaint among monogamous couples.

Sometimes problems with sex between partners can be improved when other issues, such as communication or underlying unresolved problems in the relationship, are addressed. If sex improves after such treatment, great. Often, however, sex needs to be directly addressed with specific sex therapy protocol, regardless of the initial causes of sexual problems. Sex therapists have hundreds of hours of specialty education and training in addition to licenses and degrees, and are qualified to assess and treat sexual problems. CNM clients who present with sexual issues have more complicated situations than do monogamous partners and ought to consult a certified sex therapist at least once as part of treatment.

To help CNM partners with sexual issues, clinicians can undertake the following:

- Assess sexual knowledge and practices and facilitate discussion regarding safe sex and pregnancy.
- Assess and facilitate discussion about safety and emotional security in sex practices, including alternative sex.
- Assess levels of each individual's self-esteem and personal security; work to improve these as needed.
- Determine if partners are in CNM and sex practices by choice; does anyone feel pressured or concerned about losing a partner? If partners are honestly willing, are sex practices *enjoyed* by all?
- Discern whether compatible sex practices exist between all respective partners. Are sexual interest differences one of the reasons for the CNM relationship?
- Make appropriate referrals when sexual issues are not solved by general therapeutic techniques and approaches, or when resolving other issues does not resolve sexual complaints.

References

Conley, T. D., Matsick, J. L., Moors, A. C., & Ziegler, A. (2017). Investigations of consensually nonmonogamous relationships: Theories, methods, and new directions. *Perspectives on Psychological Science, 12* (2), 205–232.

Conley, T. D., Moors, A. C., Ziegler, A., & Karathanasis, C. (2012). Unfaithful individuals are less likely to practice safer sex than openly nonmonogamous individuals. *The Journal of Sexual Medicine, 9*, 1559–1565, doi: 10.1111/j.1743-6109.2012.02712.x.

Frankl, V. Available at: www.brainyquote.com/quotes/viktor_e_frankl_160380

Gentry, E. (2016). *Forward-Facing Trauma Therapy.* Sarasota, FL: Compassion Unlimited.

Klein, M. (2017). The sex lives of engineers (and other humans). *Sexual Intelligence blog.* Retrieved August 29 from www.martyklein.com/sex-lives-engineers-humans

Kleinplatz, P. J., & Moser, C. (Eds.). (2006). *Sadomasochism, powerful pleasures.* New York: Harrington Park Press. Co-published as *Journal of Homosexuality, 50* (2/3) (2006).

Lane, A. (2015). No pain, no gain: *Fifty Shades of Grey. The New Yorker,* February 23 & March 2 issue. Available at: www.newyorker.com/magazine/2015/02/23/pain-gain

Lehmiller, J. J. (2015). A comparison of sexual health history and practices among monogamous and consensually nonmonogamous partners. *The Journal of Sexual Medicine, 12* (10), 2022–2028.

Orion, R. (2007). *Polyamory and the bisexual marriage.* Research report. San Francisco: Saybrook Graduate School and Research Center.

Orion, R. (2008a). *From traditional to open marriage.* Case study report. San Francisco: Saybrook Graduate School & Research Center.

Orion, R. (2008b). Polyamory as treatment for low desire. Paper presented at the Western Regional Conference of the Society for the Scientific Study of Sexuality, San Diego, CA, April.

Orion, R. (2011). Examining definitions and treatments of low desire and low-sex marriage (Doctoral dissertation). Available from ProQuest Dissertations and Theses Global database (Dissertation No. 3465923).

Weitzman, G.D., Davidson, J., Phillips, R., Fleckenstein, J., & Morotti-Meeker, C. (2010). *What psychology professionals should know about polyamory.* Baltimore, MD: National Coalition for Sexual Freedom, Inc.

Case Excerpt: Annika

Annika is aged 44 and lives in a middle-class suburb. She got married because "I loved the man and I wanted to be with him for the rest of my life. We'd been together for 3 years." After 2 years, Annika and her husband, Peter, decided to open their marriage.

Annika is one of my research interview subjects. The sentences in italics are my questions and comments. This is Annika's story in her own words.

Why did you decide to have an open marriage?

Peter was bisexual and wasn't interested in having sex with me any more. When we first got married, he knew about his interests, I didn't know. He didn't come out until a year into the relationship; prior to that it was a deep, dark secret. And that secret was probably the most difficult part of our relationship. So when he came clean and told me what was going on, I loved him enough to understand why, to see that he was hurting and it's not just something that he was choosing to do for fun. It was really a big burden. I thought that maybe if I could accept him, then he could accept himself.

But even after he told me, unfortunately, I don't think he was able to deal with it without blaming me for ruining our relationship. Maybe for not being a man. It was easy for him to hurt me, avoid any intimacy with me, by saying things like, "Your hair's not right," or "You've gained a few pounds," or "You're not sexual enough." There's all kinds of things that he was pushing over on me. He was feeling bad about going out with men, but instead of telling me about it even though I accepted and knew it, he lied about it! He wasn't a good liar. I think if he'd come clean and acted honestly about where he was going, we could have actually made it work. All that dishonesty was too much to handle. It was not fair and right to me.

Peter was molested when he was 17. It's something he told me about before we were married. I made allowances in the sex department because of that, too. He was married before and had three kids—whom his ex-wife doesn't let him see, I feel that's wrong. But he was going after men. So that's what broke up his first marriage. The night he told me what he was doing [going out with men], I first thought it was a provocative thing to say because he obviously likes women—because he's with me! But I soon realized it was true, of course. The more time he spent with men and the less with me, for some reason the more angry he became at me for being there. He was pulling me in and pushing me away at the same time, which was difficult.

The bisexuality I could deal with. It was the lies and the deception. I gave and gave for him to be happy. Watching your husband go off to be with other people and get sex, to go out on the town, is a hard thing to watch when you don't have it. When you're prevented from having it.

So that's what eventually brought us to counseling, and when that didn't help much [because he was hiding a lot of problems], we tried to open the marriage. It took my husband a while to become comfortable with the situation. He was turned on by it and turned off by it at the same time, it seemed to me, which is odd, I can't quite get my head around it. He thought it was the best thing for our marriage but at the same time he was very confused.

It sounds like you both tried to make the opportunities equal for both of you?

Yeah, it felt more fair to me, why should it be only him who gets the fun and sex? I was trying to explore, and it's not something I do easily. I don't sleep around and I never have, so finding someone else was stepping outside my normal little box.

So how did you find somebody else you wanted to see?

Online. I was very clear—in the body of the profile I described myself, I didn't put a picture. I just said I have this deal with my husband. The first week I got something like 80 emails because when a woman goes on a site like that and wants sex, everybody is all over it. And I didn't even put a picture! I did connect with a guy who actually did not send a picture either, we connected by email. We had a lot of things in common and he was the first person I'd ever talked to about a lot of things. He became very important—Carl.

Why was he acceptable, compared to other people?

We just connected. And because he was in a similar situation as I was—I didn't want a single guy because I didn't want the pressure of him wanting more, but, on the other hand, I needed to be sure that I liked the person. This is not my normal thing so I needed enough time to be sure of who he was and what he was doing.

He had a bisexual marriage also?

No, his wife just wanted a companionate marriage and they had children. They had the unspoken agreement—don't ask, don't tell kind of thing. He wanted to go to counseling but she didn't and she just wasn't interested [sexually] any more. He finally decided he could manage without needing her in that way, because he loves her and his family. He was just going to do without. His wife realized he was unhappy, though, and let him know he could find sex with some- one, but then she never spoke of it again. I thought that was a very nice thing. Even after my marriage fell apart, Carl never pressed me for more of a relation- ship, he is committed to his family.

Do you have children?

No, but a previous marriage. And the biggest lesson for me has been figuring out that, again, the guy I fell in love with is not the guy I married. Peter was not a guy that would lie to me, but he became that guy. I don't know if it's part of his personality to change from being one way to another. He's very charming, very good-looking, very affectionate kind of person when you meet him. Easy for him to get a woman. So I wonder if he can turn it on for a while and then he gets really restless.

Was he comfortable with his bisexuality? It sounds like the way he handled it, or his previous wife handled it, caused problems in the first marriage.

Yeah, well, they were two of a kind in some ways, stubborn. And when we were together he became *born again*, I guess you'd call it. The way his behavior changed is really mindboggling. I had accepted him for who he was. And to me, if you're a Christian, I think there is something about accepting people, and I had always thought he's one of those who accepts people all over the place! Then *he* becomes a Christian and he blames me for accepting him, his bisexual- ity, and that was not right, that I was a "sinner" for accepting him. He still is very confused.

I learned a lot about myself through this. Would I have married him had I known how it was going to end? Probably not, but, would I have married him if it hadn't ended like this? Yes, of course I would. You know, that part of it [marrying him], I don't doubt that I did the right thing.

It sounds like he was supportive of the open marriage, supportive of you having equal right to other partners, and that it was even partly his idea?

Yes and no. He was talking about a threesome with another person, another man. But I couldn't go there. I accepted the fact that he was having sex with men, but having to be *present* when he was having sex with men is not part of the deal. That was just uncomfortable for me. So he kept bringing that kind of thing up a lot and then we did start talking about opening up the marriage.

There was a group of women I found who were chatting about their open marriages. The first time Peter and I talked about it, I felt, *I can't do that*. But as our situation got worse, I realized I had to do something. I was going on 40, I wasn't ready to stop having a sex life. It's hard when you have somebody that you love and there is absolutely nothing you can do to turn them on. I mean, I would streak around the house naked and he would not react. So what do you do?

I started feeling really bad about myself. This is where that group, women all married to bisexual men, really came in. There are a lot of them out there. To everyone in that support group, partners who lied about it was the biggest thing. And the people in the group who talked openly in their marriages, they were the happiest by far. I'd much rather just say, "This is my lover and my husband and I have an open marriage, and this is what it is." That would have been fine.

It should be nobody's business, but you have to tell other people something, too. If people know you and they care about you, they want to hear something, to know that everything is all right. After my marriage broke up, I had to tell everyone, my friends and family, what had been going on. Nobody had any idea. That's how normal things looked to the outside world. The more normal it looks to the outside world, probably the more damaging it is to the people on the inside. People are constructing fake lives.

Most people have been very supportive, once I told them, saying, "Oh, I had no idea, that's amazing," or something. Even my very closest, dearest friends, who had no idea this was going on, when I told them that I had gone onto a website to look for a lover, they just . . . "You did what??" They were totally stunned. But now that they know that side of me, and what was happening, nobody has been unaccepting or judgmental.

In the aftermath, how did your parents react when you explained that your husband had difficulties, or that he had changed?

I told them that he was bisexual and they wrote him off. I don't need the support from them in that respect, I have enough from other friends. My gay friends, they have nothing to do with my husband, and he's completely different.

What are the boundaries involving time, health, commitments? You were just talking about one of them [during a tape change], if he stayed out, you at least wanted that phone call so that you would know that he was OK. Did you create additional agreements like Friday night is your night, for example, to have sacred time?

We made some initial decisions and rules for how this was going to work and decided on things together. We were agreeing to one Saturday night a month where he could go do his thing and I could go do mine, so nobody would sit here obsessing. That was the idea. I would have been fine with it, but he would go five nights out of seven. After work, he'd go pick someone up and he wouldn't tell me where he'd been, but it was so obvious. He was such a bad liar. It doesn't make any sense. Plus, the more he was lying to me, the more controlling he became on what I was doing. I had to have my cell phone on at all times, and I'd go to the gym at night and he'd say, "So where've you been, where've you been?" Well, I was at the gym! I go every night! We joined together, so, you know, where were you?

I could tell he'd come home, canceled his plans and gone off and done his thing. I even called to see if he was where he said one time, because I had a message for him. He had never been there. Then he comes home and I'd say, "So, how was the meeting?" "Oh, it was great!" You know? But with him you don't have to become a German shepherd, a dog, to sniff out clues to prove that he's lying. That snooping is just so damaging to a relationship. I don't want to be that because it affects me as well.

I accepted him and yet he would just say, "Oh, yeah, I'm not going to do that any more, I've gone to this place [to have sex with strange men], I've done it too much, I'm going to stop doing it." I had heard it a million times. It was totally detrimental to his health.

Most people in open agreements are very concerned about health.

Yeah, and you know, he's HIV positive so he can't be doing that kind of stuff. He can't be taking drugs and having random sex. But he kept doing it. He got really sick one time, and had a terrible headache, almost paralyzed on one side and his shoulder is kind of hanging, like he had a stroke. The doctors were assuring us it had nothing to do with the HIV thing, which from what I read was probably true, so what else was it? We went to expert after expert, finally we had to go to a throat expert, because he lost his vocals, one vocal chord was damaged. The doctor asked him if he had taken any kind of chemicals and Peter admitted he was doing poppers. And he'd sworn to me that he wasn't doing that. I tore my heart up trying to help him and I'm worried sick—and it's self-inflicted! He says, yeah, he's going to stop, but that stuff has a very distinct odor. I come home from work and walk into his little office where he's been playing on his computer and it smells like that stuff ["poppers"]. I'm not his mother, or the police, I'm his wife. I didn't want to do that any more. This risky behavior and endangering other people too—that's what I eventually couldn't accept when I saw he was never going to stop.

He sadly has multiple issues—substance abuse and trauma from early sexual abuse. Whether or not anybody is bisexual or in an open relationship, those issues could destroy a marriage.

I'm in touch with him and he still can't accept himself. If religion makes him peaceful, then good, I just don't think it's realistic to him. He was never at peace. But I didn't give up easily. The thing is that's what he thought was going to happen— that I'd give up and people would put him down. But when people did find out about his orientation, there was not one that did put him down, because that's not the kind of friends we have, you know? They are loving and accepting people.

I'm sad our marriage failed and look back to when we met. We did fall in love with each other and when my first marriage fell apart, Peter was there 100% to help me get myself back on track again. He said in an email the other day that that was the best year of his life, so, there you have it. We meant something to each other. But we didn't have all the answers we needed. He needs help he won't look for. It would require some very mature people, people that were very secure of themselves, I think, to make the open marriage work. People who are not obsessive and jealous.

Jealousy is not part of who I am. I mean, you'd rather have the person that you love be with you, but I was at least opening up . . . could I do it again under better circumstances? I probably would try something like that again. If I ever get into another relationship, and God I hope it's not with a bisexual man because it's just too much trouble, but you know finding something unusual or an alternative is not a problem for me. I wouldn't do it unless there is a reason for it, I wouldn't open a marriage just for fun. I think it's too dangerous. I know I'm a monogamous type of person—I like just one person at a time; actually sleeping with more than one person in separate relationships is too confusing. I have to concentrate on that one person and if it doesn't work out, I can do something else. But if Peter and I had not tried the open arrangement, we would have ended sooner. We got a divorce, but at least we gave something a try.

You found someone who helped you—the man you met?

Carl's fantastic. He wasn't the reason Peter and I divorced. We got divorced because we couldn't fix our marriage, and because Peter was out of control. I went out and had sex with a guy one time—that was it, and Carl and I just became good friends. That had nothing to do with our divorce. If my husband had been healthier and were to follow the agreements that we made, it might have worked. But of course I can't know. I can only know what I experienced.

I've learned an awful lot about human sexuality, and the way that different relationships work. One of the guys in a support group was in a relationship for 20 years with the same man, who died of AIDS. Every time he talks about it, his eyes well up and he's really sad, but at the same time he told me that they had an open relationship in their marriage because he was also in love with his wife.

I learned for myself that I could definitely sleep with somebody I wasn't in love with, and it was OK. And I feel good about that. So it's not I'm too traditional, I just know that I don't want to be with more than one person at a time, it's not necessarily the sex part, it's that for me it's too damn confusing, and I don't have that much time in my life! The liberating thing for me right now is that I don't have to get married to somebody else, I don't have to get into another relationship, I actually like living by myself. I'm not going to have kids with anybody, so there's no reason to live in a family thing, so I can build whatever kind of relationship I want. I don't know what kind of form it's going to take, it's going to depend on the person that I meet, but it's very interesting.

It sounds like your agreement with Peter, had it continued, was that you were never going to meet each other's lovers?

I think that would have been perfectly fine with me. It would have been perfectly fine with Carl, too, he would have had no problem with that. But it would have never worked for my husband. If he had been able to handle it . . . I do think that a successful open marriage is possible, but not given the situation we had . . . it does require a certain personality.

One thing that people don't get in my circle, they say, "How can you love your husband and at the same time go out with another man?" I learned that love is not a trap, it expands you. Hate contracts you but love expands you, so, you have one child and you have a second child, you don't stop loving the first child, you grow and include more people. That's a good thing. The day I went and had sex with my other guy, I drove to meet him and I must admit I felt so much love towards my husband, that he would let me do this. One love doesn't exclude another love.

But if you're lying about it and hiding the affair, then it can take away from the other one. And, of course, time is an issue, if you have two relationships going, you have to be responsible to both, you have to spend time on each one. So maybe time is being taken away from each person. But you can get jealous from work schedules, too, it's not just relationships.

If you could give advice to someone in an open relationship, or about being married to someone who is bisexual, what would it be?

Get support. Don't think you have to be alone to feel your own burden. I mean there are people out there, support groups on the internet, and there are physical [in-person] support groups as well. Because you just have such a feeling of isolation that you need to share it. Doing it without support is probably the most difficult thing.

I was in one group of women who had been in these kind of relationships for years and were very supportive, and they had found ways to make it work. Others came into the group who just found out that their husband was gay and felt their lives were falling apart, so these other women were giving them at least an option: You can stay married, you don't have to split up your family . . . this is how you could deal with it [opening the sexual aspect].

Some people don't make it, like in our case, and there's a group I was part of that people support each other through separation and the issues that come up around that. They all say in these groups, "Oh, I'm so grateful there is somebody else out there who is going through the same thing." They have nobody to talk to. And even a lot of therapists are not up on what is going on, they don't know how to help bisexual or open marriages. So there's a double whammy! People in the groups were afraid to admit their situation to their therapist and others just didn't try. So we all were therapy for each other. But you know, some people were really suffering.

This is why when you asked if I would help you and give you an interview, the reason is I think, if you write something other therapists read, they'll be educated about what's going on out there, because I think actually you're right. I saw in this support group that they didn't have therapists who thought opening *any* marriage was right. "Oh, you just have to suck it up, or get divorced, and that's the only option that there is."

Did other women in the group have a lover, as their bisexual husbands did? Is that something some of the couples were trying to make the situation work?

Some of the people are, most of the women would. There are a few who just said, "Well I haven't had sex in 25 years. No big deal, I don't care."

And some people don't.

Right. But when you used to like sex and you live with a man long enough who's not attracted to women, well, at least I eventually got to feeling I wasn't good enough, and this is where these women really need support—to know it's not them. "Oh, you turned your husband gay? You're that bad?" I heard all kinds of crazy things! Other people have told me, "I really admire you for trying that, I don't think I could do it, but I wasn't walking in your shoes."

10 Families and Consensual Nonmonogamy

Who comprises a family? According to Jim Butcher, actor and author, a family is not about "whose DNA has recombined with whose. When everything goes to hell," a family is made up of "the people who stand by you without flinching" (Butcher, 2007).

In 2010, I interviewed a young woman who had grown up in a "hippie-poly" family. While her life had not been usual, she was in the process of getting her doctorate when I met with her, so clearly her alternative family life had not impeded her academic focus or success. "One of the things I remember most is that my mom and dad grew beansprouts in an old bathtub in the basement. Oh, it was clean and all, but I really avoid eating sprouts now!"

I had asked this woman, Judy (named after Judy Collins, she was told), if there were memories that stood out for her of growing up in a less traditional family. I wondered if I'd hear some traumatizing stories, but I did not.

She was not without effect from living in a polyamorous family. She was exposed to affection displayed among three parenting partners at home. When older, she was sometimes aware of who was having sex with whom, on what night (from comments and noticing who went into which rooms). She witnessed conversations and arguments between not two but three adults about a myriad of issues common to marriage and family life. Instead of schedules and discussions about when two parents might have a night out, or when family meals could be shared, Judy's experience included three adults communicating about these things.

> Of course, I knew my family wasn't usual. A few of my mom and dad's friends knew that our live-in family friend, whom we affectionately called Uncle Bill, was actually an equal partner in my parents' threesome. Even if my mom hadn't explained to me that most people wouldn't understand, I just knew that I shouldn't talk about the real truth. It kind of made me feel left out, different, at school. But inside I always knew that no one else knew, so I was safe. All three of my parents absolutely protected me. As an adult, I see the necessity in that, but I also think it's wrong that people have to hide who they love.

Sounds a bit like having to hide an LGBTQ committed parenting relationship, when that was dangerous to reveal (still is for some people). The next children's book to follow *My Two Dads* (Harrington & Persico, 2015) may have to be *My Mom Has Two Husbands*.

Does Secrecy in CNM Protect the Child?

Judy grew up a few decades ago when polyamory was less visible and seldom reported. Her family's decision to keep their poly structure closeted was likely wise. Acceptance of and research on open and alternative lifestyles and families of any kind took a dip between the 1970s and the mid-1990s. This may have been due to the advent of HIV/AIDS, which caused a social backlash against anyone not heterosexual and western culture traditional. Dossie Easton and Janet Hardy released their book, *The Ethical Slut*, in 1997. This book sold worldwide and reopened interest in and positive public attention to consensual nonmonogamy. Since then, dozens of journal articles, books, and blogs have joined the fray and research continues to grow on CNM and on poly families.

Across the literature it is well documented that polyamorous and other consensually nonmonogamous persons face social derision, lack of effective professional help, and legal opposition. CNM practitioners who aren't secretive and selective in whom they trust may lose jobs, friends, and church acceptance, and may even be closed out by family. Children in such families may be the recipients of negative attitudes, manipulative behaviors, and bullying.

Lawsuits are known of attempts to declare poly parents unfit by outraged grandparents and other parties who take it upon themselves to "protect" the children of these nontraditional families. If CNM partners seek clinical help, they may be faced with judgment and a therapist who knows less about CNM than the clients. The current climate is improving, but those in CNM relationships or lifeways must evaluate their position:

> Depending on where you live, being openly poly could be a big deal or not a problem. A very conservative area might not be a good environment, may cause some problems with polyamorous folk, and could put your children at risk. I wish it were otherwise, but that's the simple truth. You need know how you're going to handle the risks and weigh the benefits before you explain being poly to your child.
>
> (CNM client)

Judy's family situation represents some common themes and issues in poly families. No one made fun of her having three parents because no one knew. Her parents were open about their triad at home, but according to Judy's report, they knew to keep their mouths shut to anyone outside their immediate family (whether "family" was blood kin or not). Certainly they felt that for Judy's protection, their lifeway had to be kept from public school personnel.

Secrecy about being a polyamorous family is not always the best policy, however, despite possible dangers and stigma. Children carry a burden if in a position of keeping family secrets; they may be put in a situation inappropriate for their age if circumstances arise where they have to make a decision about what to say. Believing that being secretive is normal, they may also be vulnerable to others who might want them to keep secrets.

Judy did not experience this problem, but she told me that by the time she was a teenager, her parents had come out to family and some of their friends. Once she was in high school, her family's involvement in PTA or student activities was low; she did not experience open questioning about or derision aimed at her family.

Those who oppose CNM cite the "dangers" of consensual nonmonogamy, which are the same as those cited against single parents, interracial, mixed religious, and LGBTQIQ parents:

- Children will be confused by inappropriate or immoral adult relationships.
- Children will be exposed to inappropriate sexual activity.
- All children need a female mother and a male father.
- Children will not be accepted by peers if their parents are "different."

Are Children of CNM Parents Confused by "Inappropriate" or "Immoral" Adult Relationships?

The most common form of family in America is the blended family. The most common relationship style is serial monogamy—one monogamous relationship after another, often peppered with illicit affairs. It follows that most children are exposed to more than one set of parents—more than one mom or dad and set of extended relatives, often including stepsiblings.

As a family scientist and therapist, I believe that living with contentious parents who fight or are cold to one another is more damaging to children than is seeing their parents separately, in peace. Children are capable of understanding that adults can find love with more than one person in life, and that such changes and additions are not a failure of the child (although children may need help through appropriate discussion to sort things out). Neither must this mean that a child's family gets dissolved just because the romance is gone from parents' lives.

When, why, and by whom children are informed, and what they are told, are the determining factors of whether or not children are confused or harmed by any family circumstance and situation. Children in monogamous families are exposed to confusing and upsetting adult behaviors and problems. There is no evidence that CNM families are any more or less able to appropriately inform and protect children. To the extent that communication, honesty, awareness, and concern are greater necessary factors in CNM families, such children may have better models and less inappropriate exposure. Whether consensual nonmonogamy is immoral in and of itself is a theological, social, and subjective question that is not what this book is about. Children do not believe themselves or their families to be wrong or inferior unless taught so by significant authorities.

Are Children of CNM Parents Exposed to Inappropriate Sexual Activity?

Judy's parents lived in a polyamorous triad where all adults cared for and about her. CNM folk are no more likely than monogamous partners to give children inappropriate information about or exposure to adult sexuality. Many a divorced monogamous parent has introduced a date or new love interest to the children. Others are reticent to let children know of any potential new partner until that new person is likely to become part of the family. CNM parents make the same choices.

Swingers and CNM partners with lovers who don't come to the household may not be seen by children nor impact their lives. Children don't need to know about such partners. Some CNM practitioners are glad for their children to grow up knowing that there are many ways to love and to be involved honestly with multiple partners. These values are not imparted through inappropriate exposure to adult sexuality.

Could an additional partner in a CNM family be an abuser? General statistics would say yes, it is possible, but there is no evidence that it is any more possible than in a traditional household (where the perpetrator may be a parent, step-parent, relative, or trusted family friend). There are reasons to believe that abuse would be less likely in a CNM household: A non-biologically related partner could be the one to notice and stop one of the others from perpetrating abuse. Sexual abuse does not happen in the light of day; secrecy is required. Persons who are embracing a less accepted and alternative lifeway may be more aware of and work to espouse communication skills among all family members.

Judy reported no inappropriate sexual behavior toward her, nor that she was exposed to anything she felt as traumatizing. She did express feeling "weird" knowing that her parents weren't like most other people, and she did become aware as she got older that "Uncle Bill" was more than an "uncle" in the family.

> More than once I saw mom or Uncle Bill come out of what I thought of as my parents' bedroom. Uncle Bill had his own room and used the guest bathroom as his, I never had to use a bathroom with men. I was luckier than my friend from middle school, Josie—she was in a family of five and had two brothers and they had one bathroom in their whole house! She used to come over to do her hair in my bathroom sometimes (laughs). Anyhow I asked my mom one day, I think I was about nine?, why Uncle Bill had been sleeping in her and daddy's room. Looking back, I realize she and Uncle Bill were in robes and they looked at each other knowingly in the hall when I saw them and asked that. Mom was cool about it and told me it was OK, that she and Uncle Bill were good friends, that daddy didn't mind if he took naps with mommy sometimes. As I got older and realized they must be having sex, ya, I was grossed out in a kid kind of way, but I knew by then everyone did love each other, and I loved Uncle Bill. He was always home after school and both mom and dad worked. I wouldn't have passed math if it wasn't

for him! Or got to my soccer games. He was involved in my life and I was safe with him. Even after I figured out they were both in a romance with my mom—that's what they called it, a romance!—ya, I knew that was different than Cinderella but they were honest with me and answered my questions. I never liked Cinderella anyway!

Do All Children Need a Culturally Accepted Set of Parents?

Whether children will be harmed by being raised in a family that is created by other than a heterosexual, white, Christian couple has been a publicized social issue in many eras prior to the nuclear family ideal becoming mainstream. Concerns surrounding the issue of gay parenting are the same as those emerging with the advent of other nontraditional families. Mixed race couples, mixed religious couples, LGBTQIQ (Lesbian, Gay, Bisexual, Transgender, Queer, Intersex, and Questioning) partners, and single mothers and fathers all faced—and many still do—these issues. We can expect that the same arguments and fears will abound as honest nonmonogamy, including polyamory-based families, becomes more visible.

In the field of family therapy it is common knowledge that gay parenting has no ill effects to children that are specific to the sexual orientation of parenting adults. Single parents, sexual orientation of parents, race of parents: these are not causes of harm to children, nor do they predict that children will be harmed. What can harm children is how relationships are handled, what explanations are provided, and whether or not children are loved and cared for unconditionally. Knowledge of child and brain development offered in family therapy training makes clear that it is *how* a child is raised that makes for health and happiness.

Will Children Be Accepted by Peers if Their Parents Are Different?

To the extent that any child is not accepted for any reason, the overwhelming cause of rejection is socialization toward prejudice. Every era has its "undesirables." In western culture, it was Germans, Italians, and Japanese during World War II, LGTBQIQ in many times and places in history, people of color, the "wrong" religion, "foreigners." As the song goes in *South Pacific*, children have to be carefully taught to hate. Consensual nonmonogamists are still in line for stigma and derision, until this orientation and lifeway become understood and accepted by more people than not. CNM parents are aware of this and help their children—like all other nonmainstream parents.

Judy had felt left out at school at times, she reported, but not because of CNM:

You know how the cafeteria can be a social quagmire? Well, it was a source of embarrassment for me. [Because of the beansprout sandwiches, I wondered.] Everyone else had their "Wonder Woman" or "Dukes of Hazzard" lunchboxes, but I had re-used paper bags. This one boy always called attention to me, "What hippie food is in the bag today, Collins?!" A lot of kids didn't care, and some even had bag lunches. But when you're in 6th grade being teased can be mortifying.

This author grew up in a town that was approximately 50% Jewish in population. Many days the cafeteria was peppered with bag lunches filled with Motzah and other accepted Kosher foods. No one dared to make fun of anyone's lunch in the cafeteria with teachers present (many of whom were also Jewish), but when staff wasn't looking, there were still bullies. On the playground smaller kids got picked on, as did those who looked and did things "not like us." Judy's school memories have more to do with her parents being beansprout-growing hippies than the fact that she had three intimately involved, responsible adults raising her.

Issues and Answers in Poly Parenting

What children are told, when, and by whom, are fundamental issues of parenting in CNM. In families with parents who are consensually nonmonogamous, what little research exists (Anapol, 2010; LoveMorePolyParenting, n.d.; Orion, 2008; Sheff, 2014; Sheff, personal interview, September 23, 2017) supports my 17 years of clinical experience with CNM that there may be differences in life experience, but that problems are the same as any family might have and that children are no more likely to be harmed by growing up in this family configuration. Further, there are advantages to having more than two parenting caregivers in the house. Poly partners are often considered family and play the same role as do extended family members in traditional households:

> More adults who care means more help with child care, homework, transportation, and extracurricular activities. The more adults children have to love them, they are happier and more well-adjusted. I've seen no evidence that children with more than two happy adults taking care of them are worse off! It's like having extended family around, whom the kids love, and all of whom work together positively. If the parents are happy in their relationships, it helps the family, and happy families are good for children!
>
> (poly parent client)

Children are generally smart and intuitive but do not need a lot of information at younger ages. I recall a story about a little boy who asked his father one day, "Daddy, where did we come from?" Father immediately gets nervous and thinks, *I didn't expect the birds and bees so soon!* He launches into an awkward monologue about where babies come from. When he is finished, his son says, "That's interesting, Daddy, but where did we come from? Tommy's from China!" Keep it simple for young children.

Much advice from experienced poly parents and family members is available in books, articles, and online. A grandmother who graced my office as part of a poly family for more than thirty years understands the concept of simple explanation for children:

> For a very small child, there's always the explanation that everyone loves each other and that parenting relationships are intact ... "Mommy and Daddy love each other very much, and mommy also loves Mr. Kyle, and we all love you." The older the children are, the more complicated their questions. They are concerned about what this different family means to their own lives.

As children grow, more explanation will be needed and understood. If children grow up gradually learning about their family situation in appropriate ways, they will not be upset, because they will experience their family as normal. One woman who consulted me ran a local poly discussion group. Over time I learned her experience of telling her five children about the multiple adult partners in their home, which was influenced by the many other poly parents she had known and shared experiences with in her group:

> First, I talked with my children in daily life about my own growth, how I was expanding my life in other ways, like taking classes and volunteering. We always talked about sexuality from a positive perspective, and my kids, as they grew older, talked about marriage and relationships. I included my alternative thoughts on monogamous relationships. I was honest that I have loved many people, and that I know it's possible to love more than one person at the same time. At this point they all know that I am nonmonogamous. I am openly supportive of my partner having other loves in his life, and he knows that I do as well. The kids see us living a happy, rich life and they are happy for us. We also support the fact that their choices might be different and are legitimate. We all discuss our various lovers and dates—including scheduling and relationship agreements. It's basically matter-of-fact conversation at this point. Our kids see in us a model of honest and loving multiple partnerships.
>
> We found our children were concerned that me and their father are in the open relationship by choice—not just one of us going along with it out of fear of the other one leaving. They needed to know that we still love each other and we don't plan on going anywhere. It's freeing to be honest, and it's powerful to tell the truth and show CNM as the normal life that it is for us. Our hope has been that when the kids saw that we are happy, stable, and not lying to anyone, that they would just be happy for us. This hope has come true.

What Mary, my client, describes is teaching her children *compersion* (see Chapters 3 and 5)—a term describing concern for, and joy about, the happiness and love experienced by other partners, with their other partners. Mary hopes her children will experience compersion about her: that they will be genuinely happy about her happiness with her partners. Why wouldn't they be, since she has been a responsible parent, honest, reassuring, and has spoken intelligently about herself and her partnerships? Being a positive model who speaks truthfully at age-appropriate times is a powerful and health-fostering approach, regardless of family format.

How to become such a model, however, is not always readily apparent. Getting help with this task may be a reason for consulting a therapist. I learn from clients all the time. They often have great ideas. They may not be aware that what they have chosen to tell their child is developmentally appropriate and healthy. After a break-up, when one of three partners in a poly family moved out, my client, Nancy, told me how she explained the change to her concerned daughter:

> Rachel was upset when Aaron moved out. I explained to her that Aaron and I were four things together: friends, parents to her, we work together at the shop; and we had a romance. The only change is the romance. That's not there any more, so we're happier living apart. But we still love you, I reassured her, and Aaron will still be with you like he always was, he's going to come over a lot. He and I are still friends and we still work together. We're all still family but sometimes romance feelings go away.

Her daughter, age 7, was quiet for a moment then replied, "But isn't that sad, that the romance part is gone?" Nancy replied, "Yes, that part *is* sad."

This same scenario could happen in a monogamous marriage break-up. My experience, however, is that some poly partners try to handle conflicts and break-ups more amicably than do some monogamous partners, and that the structure of poly families lends itself to maintaining group cohesiveness even when "romance feelings go away."

To the extent that this cohesion exists specific to poly families, it may be fostered by the high communication skills demanded in CNM, and that partners work to lessen jealousy and increase comperson. Poly life may engender a generosity of feelings and a propensity toward expanded relationships and acceptance. Break-ups are still painful and cause changes, but may be amicable, and the partner may remain integrated with the family, especially when children are involved. It is also common in my experience for break-ups in CNM to be just as difficult as in monogamy, and many of the same therapeutic approaches are useful for helping partners sort issues, discuss feelings, talk with children, and make changes, including separation.

Elizabeth Sheff (2014; personal interview, September 23, 2017), researcher and Certified Sex Educator, provides virtually the only empirical research on children in poly families. Those who are subjects of her 20-year study display many advantages in their situation. While Dr. Sheff points out that her sample consists of reasonably well-off and educated participants who were able to choose inclusion in the study, advantages that might help any family, children in these families with polyamorous parents thrive with "lots and lots of attention." Parents are eased and children enriched by the "practical, emotional, financial, and logistic benefits" that these family members experience due to the number of adults involved. In periodic interviews over 20-years:

> Children and parents repeatedly talked about the many advantages of having extra adults around, from help with homework, a trusted caregiver to talk with when a parent isn't available, or as an alternative to talking with a parent when doing so doesn't feel comfortable. There's someone else around to get up with the baby in the middle of the night when others have to work in the morning . . . or another person to step in when a toddler or teenager has stressed the parent beyond their ability to cope effectively.
>
> (Sheff, personal interview, September 23, 2017)

I interviewed Dr. Sheff about the details of her research findings. These include age- and stage-dependent experiences and analysis. Overall, Sheff states, the children and young adults who have participated in her research are in "great shape." She qualifies this as meaning that they are "articulate, intelligent, thoughtful, and capable young people" whose lives are not perfect but who are "equipped to deal with life's challenges."

While young children are less aware of the larger context of their lives, teens become cognizant of, and are socially impacted by, how their families are viewed. A common experience of teens that has been shared in my office is that they struggle with adolescence and that parents find them difficult to deal with. Most fear for the safety of teenagers as they venture more into the world and expand activities from childhood and learn to become adults. I have heard concerns that if topics such as sex and relationships are openly discussed, or if teens have less than conservative information and models, that they will be promiscuous and make dangerous decisions. Clients who feel this way would likely be concerned about parents in CNM situations.

As a sex therapist and educator, I believe that an appropriately informed and guided teen is the safest one. A young person with no information, by result, cannot make an informed decision. Teens are also at risk when caregiving adults are too loose with behaviors, information, and boundaries. Most parents aren't perfect, especially with regard to sex and relationship education of their children, regardless of the number of adults who act as caregivers in the home. Informed, age-appropriate discussion is needed throughout the developmental stages of children and young people. Those in CNM families may have an advantage in that adults who are successful at multiple relationships have learned to communicate regularly about difficult topics, including the complexities of relationships. They model open but appropriate relations. Sheff (2017) reported to me that:

> Teens value the role models demonstrated by different adults in family life. Teenagers value the communication and emotional intimacy skills they built up as part of the polyamorous family style. Teens reported to me that these types of skills help them, as developing young adults, to create meaningful connections with peers, lovers, and friends. They also experience emotional

intimacy and trust with their parents, something they see lacking in many of their peers' relationships with their parents. To the kids from poly families, other kids' relationships with parents seem to be filled with suspicion, tension, and anger. Kids from poly families get tense and angry sometimes too, but they report being able to have conversations with their parents that their peers claim would be unthinkable. That level of honesty allows teens from poly families to feel close to and safe with their parents—even with the usual teenage angst. These young adults view such emotional and communication skills as a great advantage to growing up in a polyamorous family, because they discover they are able to establish emotionally intimate relationships in their own lives.

Disadvantages are also noted, including that some children feel a lack of privacy, the energy of complex relationship situations, and emotional confusion with too much supervision. Many of these advantages and disadvantages can be noted in traditional marriages with extended family—granddad or aunt is on hand to help when things are stressful, to confide in, or to provide rides to the playground and extra treats. These same family members may also interfere with parental decisions and authority, or have complicated emotional relationships that impact family life.

Some stressors to children and teens that are unique to CNM reported by Sheff (personal interview, September 23, 2017) are due to the lack of understanding and acceptance of polyamorous families: stigma, (showing affection is fine) the possibility of having to be closeted about one's family, and being powerless to change this. As with some problems experienced by adults in CNM, the most serious have to do with societal attitudes and climate. Within the studied families, children and teenagers show no risk any greater than those in currently accepted common family configurations, and do show many advantages and blessings from being in one that includes more than two loving, responsibly partnered adults.

General Guidelines for Helping CNM Parents

- Keep adult issues and intimate relationships private; provide age-appropriate and world-safe explanations to children.
- Learn what is developmentally correct throughout the lifespan for children and teens to know about relationships and sexuality. This information has been studied and is available—as a culture we just don't employ it, or provide it in schools or any other forum as it ought to be. Be proactive and learn it yourself.
- Schedule family activities and support for children and teens first—then add adult relationship time.
- Be aware of the dangers of being open at this time about CNM, and especially about live-in polyamorous partners in a household with children. Be honest, share few or no sexual details, and let the children know that we are working on being accepted (just like interracial and gay marriage). Even

young children can understand simple analogies and explanations, and can learn not to say certain things or answer questions about their family unless a parent is present.

- If a new person comes into the family as a partner, whether live-in or not, both the new partner and the child need conversations and help in maintaining family structure and stability, while getting to know the new partner. This can be likened to assimilating a step-parent.

- Listen to what children and teens have to say. They are intuitive by nature and usually smart. They need to be heard. Their concerns and questions need answers. Their needs must be prioritized (which doesn't mean they run the family). They sometimes have effective problem-solving suggestions, and even insights new to the adults!

References

Anapol, D. (2010). *Polyamory in the 21st century: Love and intimacy with multiple partners*. Lanham, MD: Rowman & Littlefield.

Butcher, J. (2007). *Proven guilty*. New York: ROC.

Easton, D., & Hardy, J. W. (1997). *The ethical slut*. Berkeley, CA: Ten Speed Press.

Harrington, C., & Persico, Z. (2015). *My two dads*. New York: Penguin Random House.

Love More Poly Parenting (n.d.) Online discussion group. Available at: https://groups. yahoo.com/neo/groups/LoveMorePolyparent/info

Orion, R. (2008). *From traditional to open marriage*. Case study report. San Francisco: Saybrook Graduate School & Research Center.

Sheff, E. (2014). *The polyamorists next door: Inside multiple-partner relationships and families*. Lanham, MD: Rowman & Littlefield.

Index